Londs 1998

*Exploring Urban History*

SOURCES FOR LOCAL HISTORIANS

# Exploring Urban History

## SOURCES FOR LOCAL HISTORIANS

*Stephen Porter*

**B. T. Batsford Ltd, London**

© Stephen Porter 1990
First published 1990

Typeset by Servis Filmsetting Ltd, Manchester
and printed in Great Britain by
Courier International, Tiptree, Essex
Published by B T Batsford Ltd
4 Fitzhardinge Street, London W1H 0AH

A CIP catalogue record for this book is
available from the British Library

ISBN 0 7134 5137 8

# CONTENTS

Contents

# ACKNOWLEDGEMENTS

No introduction of the kind presented here can include all the many sources upon which an urban historian may draw. I have tried to provide an account of those which seem to me to be the principal ones and I recognize that the choice is something of a personal one that reflects my own experience. Many friends, colleagues and archivists have helped and advised me in the use of historical sources over the years; I hope that they will not feel that their efforts have been wasted. I have also learned a great deal from my colleagues at the Survey of London and the General Editor has generously allowed me to draw upon the Survey's files for some of my examples. I am very grateful to Dr Joe Bettey, both for suggesting that I undertake the writing of this book and for his wise advice on a draft of the early chapters. Anthony Seward of Batsford showed patience and understanding, especially when the writing passed through the hiccuping phase. Above all, I am grateful to Dr Joan Thirsk and Dr Ian Roy for giving me the opportunity to learn.

My thanks are also due to Irene Goes for so accurately and speedily converting my drafts into typescript.

# Chapter One
# THE ANTIQUARIAN AND HISTORICAL BACKGROUND

In the preface to his *Firma Burgi*, published in 1726, Thomas Madox wrote 'Whoso desireth to discourse in a proper manner concerning Corporated Towns and Communities, must take in a great variety of matter, and should be allowed a great deal of Time and Preparation. The subject is extensive and difficult'.[1] A modern researcher's reaction to this dictum is probably twofold; firstly that Madox's assessment was correct, and secondly that the accumulation of an extra two-and-a-half centuries of records has increased the scale of the task very considerably since his day. The 1920s generated an infinitely greater amount of relevant paper than did the 1720s and the 1980s produced records on a scale undreamed of 60 years ago. This is attributable to a growing population, much increased levels of literacy, far greater urbanization and a burgeoning bureaucracy at national and local levels of government. Not only has there been an expansion of the kinds of records which were being produced for the pre-modern town (that is, before *c.*1800), but many new categories of records have been initiated covering aspects of urban life which went largely unrecorded when Madox was working. This produces considerable problems of selection, both for the urban historian and for the writer attempting to outline some of the available sources. Modern records often present problems of access, as well as bulk. These are not, as a rule, difficulties which face the researcher into the medieval town, whose sources are, moreover, generally of a different nature to those handled by urban historians dealing with the later periods. The records which are most accessible and most commonly used by urban historians are those that originated between the early sixteenth and the early twentieth centuries, and this book is concerned largely with the sources from this period.

Madox's interests were with incorporated communities, that is, those whose constitutions and privileges were defined in charters of incorporation received from the crown, but the possession of a particular kind of administration did not confer urbanity. Some places were given the form but did not acquire the substance of a town – or they flourished for a time before passing through a kind of urban twilight into a state which was decidedly not urban – while others did not have charters, but were towns by any other definition. The definitional quagmire is a deep and potentially treacherous one, but there is generally no great need to be sucked into it, for in most cases a community's status will not be in doubt. The essential features of a town were that it contained an unusual concentration of population and a complex economy, with a significant degree of service or industrial functions, which marked it off from other nucleated settlements. The possession of a weekly market has been taken to be a rough status guide for the pre-modern town. On this basis one tenth, or a little more, of the population in the early sixteenth century were town dwellers, by 1700 the proportion was between one-fifth and one-quarter and a century later it had risen to one-third.[2] The national censuses of the nineteenth and twentieth centuries provided more precise definitions of urbanity, although they were modified from census to census. By the middle of the nineteenth century the urban population was slightly more than a half of the total and by 1911 it had reached four-fifths.[3] Villages and districts which had no urban past were drawn into the urban mesh as suburbs or satellites of the expanding towns and cities, or as towns in their own right, although it may be difficult to establish the point at which they can be regarded as being urban communities, and the modification of their local government arrangements almost always lagged well behind such changes.

The number of incorporated towns increased during the early-modern period, albeit irregularly. The political, economic, cultural and religious uncertainties of the era of the Reformation and Dissolution, for instance, were largely responsible for an unusually high number of incorporations; 39 of the 89 charters issued in the sixteenth century were granted between 1541 and 1558.[4] In the reigns of Charles II and James II many town charters were withdrawn and subsequently reissued in modified form. Thereafter, new incorporations came more or less to a halt; Birmingham and Manchester sought acts of incorporation in 1716 and 1763 respectively, but both were politely refused.[5] On the other hand, the eighteenth and early nineteenth centuries saw the creation of improvement commissions entrusted with such responsibilities as paving, lighting and the patrolling of the streets. Those towns which were not incorporated and did not claim municipal status under some customary arrangements were under manorial control or were managed by a parish vestry. The evolutionary process was interrupted by a series of legislative measures in the nineteenth century which altered the local government framework of the towns. The Municipal Corporations Act of 1835 imposed new constitutions upon 178 of the 246 boroughs which had been investigated by the preparatory Royal Commission. It did not withdraw the charters of the remainder or of other, more minor, boroughs, which continued to function until the Consolidating Act of 1882 rescinded 106 charters. The number of municipal boroughs had risen to 313 by 1901. The 1888 Local Government Act created the status of county borough, with 61 towns so designated at first and a further 20 added by 1914.

Rather lower in the urban hierarchy were those places which were constituted as urban districts by the Local Government Act of 1894. London was excluded from these Acts. Outside the City, local administration was in the hands of the justices, parish vestries and innumerable paving, cleaning and lighting boards. The Metropolis Local Management Act of 1855 merged 56 less populous parishes into 15 district boards of works, leaving the vestries of 22 of the larger parishes as district authorities in their own right, and also established the Metropolitan Board of Works as the overall authority for such matters as main drainage, building regulations, street improvements, open spaces and, later, fire fighting. In 1889 the Board was superseded by the London County Council and by the 1899 London Government Act the former parishes and district boards were replaced by 28 metropolitan boroughs.

A charter of incorporation assured the urban community of its autonomy and the administrative consequences of such independence were reflected in the series of records which were kept. The compilation of records does not invariably result in their preservation, even if they are of an official nature, but fortunately the sixteenth and seventeenth centuries saw the development of an awareness of the desirability of securing and conserving muniments. This had a practical expression in the designation of responsibility for their care to an officer of the corporation and in the construction of a strong room or safe for their storage. In 1611 Leicester corporation paid a carpenter for 'tymber and workmanshyppe to make a conveynient roome in the towne hall to laye upp the Townes Records'.⁶ In this century a similar concern has led some towns to establish a civic record office or an archives department within a library, while others have deposited their collections in the appropriate county record office. However, a number of towns have retained their archives within their strong rooms, perhaps making access to them rather difficult. This also applies to modern records, which may still be held by the administrative departments that generated them, or their successors. For the majority of the boroughs there is a coherent collection of material which has survived and is accessible.

Other records which need to be consulted by the urban historian originated outside the boroughs' jurisdiction. This applies to parish records, for example, which, as a result of the Parochial Registers and Records Measure of 1978, are now mostly in the care of the record offices. Episcopal, capitular and archdiaconal papers are in the custody of those record offices that have been designated as the approved repositories. Other relevant material, including manorial records, is to be found in family, solicitors' or other business collections. Many such collections have been deposited in record offices, but others are still in private hands. Record offices commonly keep a list of material for their area which is held elsewhere, and its whereabouts can also be traced through the

Historical Manuscripts Commission. A listing of relevant records has to take account of the Public Record Office's holdings. The three volume *Guide to the Contents of the Public Record Office* (1963–8) provides an introduction which has to be followed up through the indeces available for the individual classes of records. Unfortunately, by no means all of the classes are indexed by place, which is clearly the requirement of a researcher investigating a particular town or district. Nevertheless, an increasing amount of material in the Public Record Office is being made accessible.

## The evolution of urban history

The writing of urban history has a long pedigree. The borough annals or chronicles may be seen as the precursors of the genre. Some of them were begun in the late fifteenth century. They survive for more than 20 provincial towns and most of them have been published. Such annals were usually compiled by the leading townsmen who were members of the governing body or had access to its deliberations or records, as the town clerk would have done, for example. They generally consist of notices of the chief events in the urban calendar, such as the civic elections, commercial negotiations and agreements, some of the more important council ordinances and, more rarely, significant national and international events. They may also contain lists of the chief officers of the corporation. This material was selected by the compiler from the numerous transactions of the corporation and although it may merely reflect his own interests and opinion of what was important, with care it can be interpreted as an indication of the constitutional, economic and social problems that were preoccupying the leading citizens of the town at that time. The interests of the compiler will become apparent to a researcher working on the source, but it should be borne in mind that a number of persons, with differing concerns, may have had a hand in compiling such annals.

The earliest antiquarian histories were in some ways a development from the annals, for many of them were written by those who had the custody of, or an interest in, municipal records. The younger Henry Manship's history of Great Yarmouth, published in 1619, was partly the outcome of his listing of the borough's archives.[7] Their authors were typically the corporation's officers, local gentry, prosperous citizens and clergymen. They paralleled the county histories, the first of which, William Lambarde's *Perambulation of Kent* (1576), inspired John Stow to compile his incomparable *Survey of London* (1598). Stow's *Survey* and John Hooker's *The Discription of the Cittie of Excester* (c. 1580, published in full 1919) were the first major works of this kind. Already, too, there were the beginnings of more specialized writing, some of it designed to promote a town's particular characteristic, as in *The Bathes of Bathes Ayde* by John Jones (1572). The number of antiquarian histories that appeared in print before the end of the seventeenth century was not very great, however, and indeed authors found some difficulty getting their work published. De La Pryme's history of Hull, written at the very end of the century, and Abel Wantner's early eighteenth-century account of Gloucester remain in manuscript. Sir Thomas Widdrington presented his survey of York to the city in about 1660 in the hope that the council would help to finance its publication, but was told that in the aftermath of the Civil War such an account of the city's former prosperity was unwelcome, if only because 'it seems to add to our unhappiness that our predecessors were so happy'. The work remained unpublished until 1897.[8] The timing of Widdrington's request was rather ill judged, but even so he was unfortunate to receive such a reaction from his prospective patrons. Succeeding generations generally received a more favourable response. Indeed, authors increasingly found borough corporations to be willing dedicatees, and civic pride dictated that many such bodies were not only prepared to accept dedications but also to commission histories or descriptions of their town. There was a considerable increase in the numbers of such works towards the end of the eighteenth century and they have continued to appear, with a few falterings, since then. Some volumes have been prepared to mark the anniversary of a charter or other significant date in a borough's history. The 1972 Local Government Act, which marked the end of the separate administration of many boroughs, was a productive piece of legislation in this respect. The attention of the early urban historians was not confined to the major towns and cities and many of the smaller ones were also covered, despite the apparently rather limited market for such works. There were, for example, histories of such towns as Lowestoft (1790), Chichester (1804), Richmond in Yorkshire (1821) and Banbury (1841).[9] This is still the case, for much current research in urban history is concentrated on the smaller towns.

As well as being treated in separate histories, towns were also covered in long essays in the county histories which were produced in the eighteenth and nineteenth centuries. The county towns received particularly extensive treatment in such works. More than 600 folio sized pages of John Nichols's *History of Leicestershire* (1815) were devoted to Leicester, for example, and an entire volume on Salisbury was contributed to Hoare's *History of Modern Wiltshire* (1843). Other towns were commonly given less space, usually in a section containing parochial histories, but in many cases these were longer than any other published work then available. It is perhaps worth mentioning at this point that this is also the format that has been adopted by the Victoria County History. In the earlier volumes the towns were given comparatively little space and the coverage was disappointingly brief, but in more recent years this has been remedied and the larger towns are now allocated a separate volume, as in many of the earlier county histories.

The early histories were idiosyncratic works with few common characteristics, but in the eighteenth century something of a standard format did begin to develop and it is clear that many authors both corresponded with each other and consciously used other publications in the genre as models for their own work. They generally covered a number of themes. The development of the town's constitution and the structure of its government were commonly given considerable prominence, for they were seen as the essential basis of its identity and separateness from other communities. It was also usual to include a chronological section which not only mentioned some of the more noteworthy occurrences within the town itself, but also events that were prominent in national history, and changes of reign, although these may not in fact have had much of an impact locally. Another common feature was the inclusion of lists of the holders of the major offices and brief biographies of civic dignitaries and eminent sons of the town. Many such histories gave a great deal of space to descriptions of the churches in the town, often including numerous transcriptions of the monumental inscriptions within them, as well as lists of incumbents and a proud enumeration of the charitable bequests made by the citizenry over the years. The reader can expect to find the economic history of the town less well covered, although its trades and industries may be described, with emphasis given to those that were currently prospering. Public buildings and utilities such as the water – and later gas – supply were also thought to be suitable topics for inclusion. Such works provide not only an account of the town's history, but also a description and an impression of it when the volume was compiled.

The antiquarians' works do have their weaknesses, however. Without firm archaeological or documentary evidence for early history they tended to perpetuate the civic myths that had developed to explain the origins of a town and its privileges, such as the Lady Godiva legend at Coventry and the representation of Leicester as King Lear's capital. In other ways, too, their historical accuracy was often rather wayward and their interpretations do have to be treated cautiously. Moreover, there was a tendency for their authors to regard the past as the foundation of the present liberties and prosperity of the town, producing a rather bland effect and glossing over the often acute social problems that confronted the urban community, especially during periods of rapid population growth and, in many towns, industrialization.

There were shorter historical and descriptive entries in the gazetteers, directories and guidebooks which were published in increasing numbers during the nineteenth century. Amongst the earliest and most useful of the national gazetteers was Samuel Lewis's *Topographical Dictionary of England* (first edition 1831 – seventh edition 1849) and his *Topographical Dictionary of Wales* (first edition 1833 – fourth edition 1849). The same strictures apply to these works as to the more substantial antiquarians' publications. Their characteristics need present no great problems of interpretation to researchers, who will, in any case, be able to build up impressions from their own work to set against those provided by such volumes.

The antiquarians performed a useful service for modern researchers by collecting and transcribing documents relating to their particular town, perhaps translating items that were in Latin. Many of them included a part of their collections in their published work, both full transcripts of some documents and the authors' notes of the contents of others. Some of the histories were avowedly produced for the purpose of making such compilations generally available, as with John Boys's *Collections for an History of Sandwich* (1792) which, according to the author, consisted of 'historical facts taken from old and authentic records'. The unpublished papers of such antiquarians may have been deposited in the local record office and should be investigated for relevant material. As well as transcripts and notes, they may contain original documents. Arthur Preston's collections for Abingdon, for example, include transcriptions made for him from the public records as well as his own notes and those surviving records of the borough which his father had acquired after the corporation had disposed of them for waste paper in 1867. The Shropshire record office contains a similar deposit of material relating to Bridgnorth, derived from the public records and the borough archives.[10]

There may be some doubt about the accuracy and completeness of both published and unpublished records from such collections. Comparison of a transcript with an original which is available will quickly establish whether the former is an accurate copy that can be used with confidence, and will give a researcher some indication of the antiquarian's reliability in this respect, while the very nature of the material in the collection should show what special interests influenced its compilation. Obviously, if both are available then the original is to be preferred, unless it presents great problems of palaeography, but such collections will probably contain items which have since been lost or destroyed or are not now accessible. They can also save time and labour, for instance for researchers without easy access to the Public Record Office or other distant repositories. Moreover, they can be used to gain an impression of the nature of the material and its likely usefulness before beginning work on the original documents. It is very discouraging to work through a collection only to find that it has little or nothing of value to the research in hand.

The more professional approach to record keeping in the nineteenth and twentieth centuries was reflected in the numerous published volumes of transcripts that can be taken to be accurate. Some of these are to be found in what may be called the national series. The early volumes issued by the Historical Manuscripts Commission include reports on the holdings of almost seventy corporations and boroughs, but these are not comprehensive and tend to concentrate on the medieval period. Two reports look in more detail at the records of Beverley (1900) and Exeter (1916) and these contain fuller and more representative selections of items. Since the Exeter volume was published the Commission has not devoted a report to a collection of borough records, concentrating rather on family archives, although many of these volumes do contain information that is relevant to the urban historian and are well indexed. The Royal Historical Society's *Camden* series began in 1838 and this, too, has a few volumes containing transcripts of town records. Similarly, the record series of the Board of Celtic Studies has a volume devoted to a calendar of the Haverfordwest borough records from 1539 to 1660. Even the Selden Society's record series on the history of law contains a volume of urban records; extracts from the archives of medieval Beverley. All of these series, indeed, are likely to contain some information for the urban historian, even in those volumes which cover collections that are not urban in origin, and a browse through them may turn up helpful material to supplement that which is available from the borough collections themselves.

Far more material on urban history has been included in the record series of local societies. Many of these were established in the nineteenth century, such as the Surtees Society for Northumberland and Durham and the Chetham Society for Lancashire and Cheshire, which issued their first volumes in 1835 and 1844 respectively. Most such societies are based upon the counties, but have nevertheless issued volumes of urban records, such as those of Beverley and York in the record series of the Yorkshire Archaeological Society. There are also likely to be substantial extracts from documentary material relevant to urban history in articles in the annual transactions or proceedings of such societies. Few cities and towns have had their own societies able to support a record series, although one was begun for Southampton in 1905 and others followed at Newcastle-upon-Tyne, Bristol, Portsmouth, London and, perhaps most enterprisingly, in the relatively small town of Banbury, which issued its first volume in 1959. In addition, a number of corporations commissioned or financed publication of volumes of transcripts or extracts of their own records independently of such societies. The pride with which they did so is often apparent from the prefaces to such works. The two volumes of extracts from the Northampton records were published in 1898 by order of the town council, avowedly as a stimulus to the accurate study of local history and to civic duty.[11] Attitudes had obviously changed a great deal since the Abingdon corporation records had been thrown out. The 1890s and 1900s were fruitful decades in this respect, with series published for Reading, Nottingham and Leicester, as well as volumes for a number of other towns. This rate of output was not maintained, however, and interest in urban history passed through something of a trough before it was revived much more recently.

There can be few, if any, towns or topics in urban history for which there is no published material. The most comprehensive bibliographical guides are Charles Gross's *A Bibliography of British Municipal History* (2nd edition 1966) and the supplementary and detailed *A Bibliography of British and Irish Municipal History* by G.H. Martin and S. McIntyre (1972). Current publications are conveniently listed in the annual bibliography in the *Urban History Yearbook* (1974–). In addition, more detailed published bibliographies are available for some counties or towns. Reference libraries and record offices commonly keep fairly comprehensive collections of printed material; books, pamphlets and perhaps offprints from those journals which may not be readily obtainable outside academic libraries. Many of them have specialist local history sections with place and subject indices that enable a researcher to discover the material that is available. A reading list of published work has a value not only in revealing the topics which have been investigated and written up but also the chronology of interest in them, for research goes in phases, if not actually in fashions. This partly reflects the different objectives which succeeding generations of historians bring to the subject.

## Travellers and writers

One type of source which has attracted the attentions of publishers is the journals of travellers and tourists. For the mid-Tudor period Leland's itineraries of England and Wales are invaluable. The best known examples for the late seventeenth and early eighteenth centuries are probably those of Thomas Baskerville and Celia Fiennes, and Daniel Defoe's *A Tour through the Whole Island of Great Britain* (1724–6).[12] Amongst those for the later eighteenth century are Richard Pococke's narratives of his travels and *The Torrington Diaries*.[13] The majority of such accounts that are available are by British men and women engaged in what has been described as the 'Discovery of Britain'.[14] Those written by foreign travellers are also valuable, for they were likely to comment on features that were too familiar for the indigenous traveller to mention. They also provide comparisons with towns and cities overseas.

Travellers' accounts provide us with the writer's subjective reaction to a town, which was usually based upon a brief visit of a day or two, rather than a considered opinion that was the outcome of a certain familiarity with the place. They tended, naturally enough, to be concerned with the finer and more unusual features, while the mundane and less attractive aspects, to the contemporary eye, were ignored. It was common for visitors to be shown around by a friend or one of the town's leading citizens, who would obviously be keen to show the town off to its best advantage and avoid the less salubrious districts. The major buildings feature prominently in such descriptions, not excluding commercial premises and factories in the early period of industrialization. The nature of the visit is likely to have affected the visitor's impression, as well as the time of the year and even the weather. Similarly, the purpose for which such journals were written may have influenced their content. An account compiled largely for personal reference should have a greater degree of informality and therefore convey a truer picture of the writer's impressions than one which was produced with a wider readership in mind and even perhaps with one eye on possible publication. For that reason the earlier of such accounts generally have a freshness and candour not always found in those which were written when the genre had become a familiar one and developed a degree of self-consciousness.

Travellers tended to give their impressions of the fabric of a town, perhaps only in general terms, but this may constitute useful evidence nevertheless. Leland's note that in mid-sixteenth-century Northampton 'All the old building of the toune was of stone, the new is of tymbre' points to an interesting aspect of the town's building history.[15] Such observations may be more specific. The extent to which brick had been adopted in Norwich by the late seventeenth century is indicated by Celia Fiennes, who noticed that there were very few brick houses other than those owned by some rich factors. She also wrote that the streets there were 'all well pitch'd with small stones'. Some comment on the economic basis and prosperity of a town was also fairly typical of such narratives. Indeed, it was a particular concern of Defoe, although he was prone to exaggeration in this respect. Fiennes's description of the stagnating cinque port of Sandwich as 'a sad old Town' captures succinctly its economic condition at the end of the seventeenth century.[16] The information in travellers' writings was not only impressionistic, however, for in some cases it was based upon close observation and informed enquiry. Foreign visitors were likely to be curious about the political arrangements of towns. This was true of Alexis de Tocqueville, whose accounts of his visits in 1833 and 1835 have been published in English as *Journeys to England and Ireland* (1958). They include notes on Birmingham's administration, to the extent of including a fairly full summary of the clauses of its Improvement Act of 1828.[17]

A more intimate picture of the routines of urban life is revealed in the diaries and journals of the citizens. The best known examples must be Pepys's and Boswell's London, perhaps Anthony Wood's Oxford,[18] but there are many other less famous, if also less revealing, documents of this kind. They are, of course, coloured by the writer's view of the world and the size and nature of the circle of acquaintances in which he or she moved. Indeed, they invariably present a picture of a particular, perhaps rather narrow, section of society. This also applies to autobiographical writings. William Hickey's London is brought vividly to life in his *Memoirs*, but it is hardly a rounded view of the capital in the second half of the eighteenth century which emerges from them. His objective was an account of his life rather than a description of the city.[19] Other, less exuberant, autobiographies were more consciously aimed at a re-creation of the society in which the writer had lived. A successful example of this kind of composition is the mid-Victorian Farnham which is described by George Sturt.[20] It should be borne in mind that an autobiographical account may have been coloured by an element of self-justification or special pleading, perhaps even have been written with that purpose. An added problem in interpreting such retrospective writings is the selectivity of a writer's memory. A picture of an urban society as it was, say, 30 years before is invariably coloured by the events of the intervening years, for it required a major feat of memory and communication to accurately re-create for posterity a milieu that had passed, however slow the pace of change may appear to have been. An autobiographer may have had access to private correspondence, which also furnishes a source for the historian. Among the variety of topics typically dealt with were family concerns, business matters, the politics of the town, social events and perhaps a slant on national affairs. Even more than diaries and autobiographies, collections of letters present a partial and fragmented view of the town in question. Despite such strictures, the sources described in this paragraph are potentially of great value for the insights which they provide into the lives of individuals and in helping to balance the impersonality of many types of records, especially those of an official or semi-official nature.

A further readily accessible source which should not be eschewed is fiction: novels, stories and drama. A writer's power of description and encapsulation can give both a fine insight into the society depicted and a representation of the physical appearance of a town. Of course the intention may not have been to produce an accurate account, rather to capture the essence of the place during a particular period, and it is in this sense that the urban historian is best served. In some cases the writer had a long familiarity with the town described and has become closely identified with it. Thomas Hardy's Dorchester as described in *The Mayor of Casterbridge* is a justly famous portrayal of a market town in southern England before the coming of the railway, while the 'five towns' of Stoke-on-Trent described in Arnold Bennett's novels and short stories are a far different, industrialized, community. In other instances the town featured by a writer was drawn from impressions received during a short stay. Jane Austen's visit to Lyme Regis in 1804 provided the material for her description of the town in *Persuasion*, written a few years later, and George Farquhar sufficiently absorbed the atmosphere of Lichfield, when he was briefly posted there as a recruiting officer, for it to serve as the provincial town which is the setting for *The Beaux' Stratagem* (1707). Many works of literature of the seventeenth and eighteenth centuries were set amongst the fashionable sections of London society and tended to parody, rather than faithfully describe, the *beau monde* featured in them, sometimes unmercifully so. By contrast, George Gissing's novels portray working-class life set against the sombre, even bleak, background of late Victorian London. The nature, purpose and context of a work have to be understood. Changing literary attitudes are discussed by Raymond Williams in *The Country and the City* (1973). A writer's intentions may have been to isolate an aspect or feature in order to criticize it, directly or obliquely. The powerful social criticisms contained in Dickens's novels are a case in point. They are equally present in his journalism. The kind of journalism which is most useful to the historian is that which is directed to an end and deals with the particular issue in view. It may supply the reader with much insight into the issues and conditions of the time, yet is only a part of the jigsaw, and other sources have to be consulted before the picture can be brought to anything resembling completion.

# Chapter Two
# SITE AND LAYOUT

Personal observation and the examination of a range of maps and plans provide the basis for a study of an urban area's site and topography. Relief, geology, drainage and water supply are obviously major factors influencing the location of a town or district, and its development. These are shown on the maps of the Ordnance Survey and Geological Survey, but it should be borne in mind that not all physical features have remained unaltered in historic times. The natural drainage pattern may have been obscured by the diversion of streams and, for reasons of convenience and public health, their covering in and perhaps incorporation into the modern sewer system. Nor is relief entirely free from human modification. Terracing, levelling, infilling, draining and even some accumulations of building and occupational debris have altered the natural contours of many towns. Roman London lies at between ten and twenty feet below the present surface of the city.[1] There have also been deliberate changes in modern times, some resulting from engineering work for utilities such as railways and docks and others because of the need to alter features which restricted the expansion of a town, leading to, for example, the diversion of streams or the infilling of shallow valleys. Coastal towns are subject to changing relative sea levels, erosion or deposition, which may have modified their topography and hence their function. The medieval ports of Ravenserod and Dunwich on the east coast were both completely destroyed by erosion. The silting of an estuary may have altered the nature of a town some distance upriver, without affecting its actual site. Chester and Rye both declined as ports for this reason and their functions were changed in consequence.

Siting was determined not only by physical factors, but also by cultural ones, such as land ownership, and defence requirements. The choice of a location by a manorial lord or the Crown for the erection of a castle, or the foundation of an abbey, were important factors in medieval urban development. Many towns owe their existence to deliberate attempts at creation by the acquisition of the right to hold a weekly market and seasonal fairs. Some attempts of this kind failed and others were only partially successful, yet their legacy remains in the urban pattern. Topography imposed certain constraints on such plantations. Nevertheless, some towns established in this way do occupy rather unusual sites. A town on a hillside 650 feet above sea level and with a north-westerly aspect defies most theories of urban location, but Chipping Norton in Oxfordshire occupies such a site, because that is where, in the mid twelfth century, the lord of the manor chose to establish his new market town.[2] Industrialization, changing patterns of internal and overseas trade and communications, the commercialization of leisure and new defence conditions during the post-medieval period resulted in the creation of other new towns, some of them on wholly new sites and others expansions of small villages. Examples, of canal, spa, port and dockyard, railway and industrial towns, include Stourport-on-Severn, Southport, Whitehaven, Barrow-in-Furness, Crewe and Middlesbrough. Other sites lost their earlier importance and the towns occupying them shrank into relative insignificance.

Plans are available for all towns, from the mid nineteenth century through the Ordnance Survey's series, and most towns also have some cartographic coverage for the previous 300 years. Features which dominate the urban form can be readily identified. They include rivers, the position of bridges, the alignments of the principal streets, and perhaps of the town walls and gates. The changes arising from the addition of new streets, the development of suburbs, and the construction of the canals and railways, may also be charted. These changes have been most rapid and extensive in the nineteenth and twentieth centuries in the majority of towns – although not in those country towns which have stagnated or declined – but earlier plans should provide evidence for expansion or decline in the Stuart and Georgian periods, to use in conjunction with estimates of population size. In addition to maps and plans, air photographs can be used to study the topography of towns, both their overall geography and the character of their constituent districts.

A series of plans will undoubtedly contain some unfamiliar street names. Within the area of medieval Oxford there are 40 streets that have undergone some change of name – many of them have experienced several changes – and 14 others that have been 'lost'.[3] The later reuse of such 'lost' street names elsewhere can be a further source of confusion. The numbering of houses within streets from the late eighteenth century onwards apparently makes their identification much easier by giving each house a unique identity. Care has to be taken even in this respect, however, for the renumbering of houses has been a not uncommon occurrence. The extent and frequency with which names and numbers have been altered is indeed surprising. Although local authority lists of such changes may be available from the mid or late nineteenth century, it is, nevertheless, advisable to identify and record any changes which are encountered. This also applies to boundary changes. The Ordnance Survey's archive contains plans showing all local authority boundary changes after 1841, but it is important to note that boundaries were subject to alteration even before the administrative changes of the nineteenth and twentieth centuries.

# Early town plans

Urban cartography in the British Isles began in the late fifteenth century, and by the mid-Tudor period plans were being produced that are of great topographical value as the earliest reasonably faithful representations of towns. Plans were prepared for a variety of purposes, and the cartographer's intentions and instructions obviously affected the content of a plan, and hence its interpretation by historians. Some were designed to depict the whole of a town and were issued as individual sheets, as parts of an atlas, or to illustrate a local history, directory or guide book. Such published plans tend to be the best known and most accessible representations of towns and many of them are available as modern facsimiles. Some are aesthetically very fine productions, which enhances their appeal.

The earliest printed plan of an English town was Cuningham's 1558 panorama of Norwich, an example of a perspective, or bird's-eye, view. This style of depiction evolved first into plans on which buildings and other features are shown in three dimensions – so called plan-views – and later into the familiar two-dimensional form, with all features shown in plan to a uniform scale. Nine towns in England and Wales were included in the first five volumes of Braun and Hogenberg's *Civitates Orbis Terrarum* (1572–98), but these do not include Bristol and Newcastle, among the larger towns. John Speed's *Theatre of the Empire of Great Britain* (1611–12) has plans of 73 towns as insets on the county maps, although only 50 of them were based upon his own surveys, the remainder being derived from other cartographers.[4] Speed's atlas was the source for the plans of nine British towns included in the sixth and final volume of the *Civitates* (1617) and was also drawn upon for other publications. It was a common practice to reissue plans without revision, often many years after the original survey. A plan of Gloucester issued in Frankfurt in 1650 was essentially a reproduction of Speed's plan of 40 years earlier and so is misleading. Most of the plans in the *Theatre* were of the county towns and so very small ones, such as New Radnor, were included, while some of the larger towns were not.[5] A number of series of town plans were produced in the eighteenth and early nineteenth centuries, notably by John Rocque, and as illustrations in such works as Britton and Brayley's 18 volume *The Beauties of England and Wales* (1801–15). There were also numerous productions of individual towns and their constituent parishes and wards, for a variety of purposes.

Some cartographers were commissioned by the corporation or lord of the town, or they dedicated their plans to them in the hope of recognition and reward. They were presumably expected to produce flattering pieces of work, showing the town off to its best advantage. James Millerd's plan-view of Bristol of 1673 pleased the city council so much that it gave the cartographer its thanks and a silver tankard valued at £10 7s. 6d. It was re-issued on four occasions in the following 60 years, and the growth of the city can be traced from the successive issues.[6] Such revisions may not have been surveyed or executed to the same standards as the original, however, and in some cases the differences are so obvious that the additions can easily be identified. A map of Sherborne drawn in 1802 was derived from a plan of 1735 and shows those buildings that had been destroyed in the intervening years and not rebuilt.[7] In that instance the derivation is clear, in others it may not be so apparent, and it is important to establish the date of the actual survey on which a plan was based, or the earlier plan from which it was taken.

Many town plans have illustrations and miscellaneous information around their borders. The cartouche often incorporates the arms of the corporation or lord, having a symbolic, not merely decorative, function. Some plans carry descriptions and perhaps a brief history of the town, information on land ownership, population figures and the days on which the markets and fairs were held, for they had a promotional purpose. William Naish's 1751 plan of Salisbury was dedicated by his printer to the bishop of that diocese and carries the annual list of preachers at the cathedral. Such plans may not, of course, be the only extant sources for that kind of information and historical accounts attached to such plans should, in any case, be treated circumspectly. Naish's plan also has a view of Salisbury cathedral from the south-west and a 'prospect' of the town taken from the opposite direction. It was fairly common for cartographers to provide illustrations of individual buildings and a perspective view of the town from a low angle, designed to portray a visitor's impressions when approaching it. The plan of Manchester and Salford produced by Casson and Berry in 1745 has a perspective view of this kind, an illustration of the early eighteenth-century St Ann's Square, the elevations of 16 of the principal buildings, a fulsome description of the town and even a plan 'taken about 1650' as an inset. Not all town plans have quite so much extra material, but this example provides some idea of the range of information that they may carry.

In addition to the reasons outlined above, town plans were also produced because of incidents which had aroused particular interest. Military actions led to the preparation of a number of plans. One of the earliest of these depicts Brighton at the time of a French raid in 1545, during which the town was burnt. Maps of several towns were produced during the civil wars of the mid-seventeenth century and the Jacobite rebellions of the eighteenth, to illustrate sieges – such as those at Newark (1645), Colchester (1648) and Carlisle (1745) – or battles, for example at Worcester (1651) and Preston (1715). They were hastily issued to satisfy the public interest stimulated by such operations and so their evidence should be treated with some caution. Military considerations led to the preparation of plans of the fortified coastal towns and these are rather more dependable. The earliest plans of Portsmouth (*c.* 1540) and Berwick (*c.* 1575) were drawn up for military purposes, and because of the continuing interest of military engineers such towns have been particularly well covered cartographically. Their growth was greatly influenced by their fortifications. Even the 'temporary' defences of inland towns constructed during the Civil War proved to be expensive and difficult to remove, influencing the topography of a district for many years. The large fort known as the Queen's Sconce at Newark still survives, on land which has remained undeveloped, but even in a built-up area such as the Whitechapel district of London the remains of a Civil War fort were still prominent at the end of the eighteenth century, when a plan of them was compiled.[8]

Plans were also produced after some of the major urban fire disasters, to show the extent of the damage and to plan the rebuilding. The most notable example is Hollar's plan of London after the Great Fire. Others include one which was produced after a blaze had destroyed almost all of Blandford Forum in 1731, which showed the area destroyed and also carried a description of the fire. The 'Correct Ground Plan of the Dreadful fire at Ratcliff' was issued after a fire had burnt down more than 450 houses in east London in 1794. There are relatively few such plans, but those which do exist are especially valuable because they illustrate the district affected at a point of substantial and enforced change in the townscape.

Most towns had been covered by a general plan of some kind by the end of the eighteenth century. Amongst the exceptions were some small country towns and a few more surprising cases. Taunton, for example, was featured in a small street plan on an inset to a map of the surrounding area in 1791, but not until 1840 was a detailed plan of the town produced. It was, however, the county town of Somerset and its population, almost 6,000 in 1801, more than doubled in the first half of the nineteenth century. Size and status did not in themselves guarantee that a cartographer would be found to produce a plan of a town: there had to be sufficient commercial incentive as well, and Taunton had failed in that respect, for proposals issued in 1782 did not attract anything like the required number of subscribers and so the project was not carried through.[9]

Town plans of the pre-modern period do have to be interpreted with caution. The earlier ones were clearly imprecise, for surveying techniques had not been perfected, and it should not be assumed that those produced in the eighteenth and early nineteenth centuries were accurately surveyed. Moreover, the cartographer did not always represent topographical features as they actually were when the plan was surveyed. There was a very strong temptation, which arose from commercial need, to produce as up-to-date a plan as possible, to the extent of showing proposed developments as if they had taken place, although in the event they may not have been executed as planned, or even executed at all. This applies especially to canal and railway schemes, but also to new streets, housing developments and even such features as pleasure gardens. Milne's 1791 plan of Southampton depicts wharves and a canal which were never constructed, and the 1813 edition of Horwood's plan of London shows Regent's Park as then proposed, which was quite different from the park that was actually laid out.[10] The tendency to anticipate new developments makes such plans rather dubious sources from which to date such changes with accuracy.

## County maps, road atlases and coastal charts

Towns which do not have individual cartographic coverage before being surveyed for the Ordnance Survey are nevertheless shown on county maps. The earliest such maps are of little value to the urban historian, for they are on too small a scale to be useful and tend to show towns by means of conventional symbols. Those produced in the eighteenth century are more helpful, however, for the standard of surveying improved and there was a tendency to adopt larger scales. In 1759 the Royal Society of Arts offered a prize of £100 to cartographers producing county maps of sufficient merit at the one inch to the mile scale, and this proved to be a considerable stimulus, with many counties being resurveyed in the following years.[11] It became a fairly common practice to issue such maps in atlas form and this was also done in the case of road maps. Specialized road maps began with John Ogilby's strip maps at one inch to the mile in his *Britannia* (1675). The format was copied by a number of later cartographers, notably by John Cary (*c.* 1754–1835), who surveyed post roads for the government and produced strip maps which can be regarded as reliable. Towns cannot be given detailed coverage at the scales adopted for such maps, even those at the one-inch scale, but their size and form are clearly recognizable and Ogilby's maps do provide useful cartographic evidence for those smaller towns that were not to be surveyed until a much later date.

Coastal charts provide evidence of a similar nature. British marine cartography began in the reign of Henry VIII, with military considerations providing the stimulus. On some charts of the coastline the landward area was left blank, but on others coastal towns and villages were shown. Because such charts were designed primarily to show the shoreline and off-shore features, the towns depicted on them may not be illustrated accurately or in very much detail. Nevertheless, they do provide early plans of some towns, such as the bird's-eye view of Dover on a chart of the harbour dated 1595.[12] As with other branches of cartography, the standards of surveying steadily improved and the more accurate of the later two-dimensional plans on coastal charts can supply good cartographic evidence for the urban historian.

# Estate maps

Estate maps form the largest category of unpublished cartographic material available to the researcher. There are some early examples from before the mid-sixteenth century, but the really rapid expansion of property surveying began during the Elizabethan period and such maps became numerous after *c.* 1700. They illustrate the estates of private owners, large and small, the Crown, the Church, borough corporations, the guild and livery companies and charitable land. The coverage ranges from entire towns to plans of individual buildings. Some small towns, such as Warwick and Sherborne, were in the hands of a single owner and so were surveyed in their entirety. This also applied in the case of Walker's 1591 survey of the manors of Chelmsford and Moulsham and Pettis's survey of the parish of St Ives, Huntingdonshire, of 1728; in both instances the towns were shown on maps of much larger areas. It was much more common for urban property to be in multiple ownership, the results of the vagaries of inheritance, purchases and sales, and gifts.

Estate plans may be on individual sheets with supplementary information on tenants, rents and the condition of the properties around their borders, or in volumes, with such data on facing or adjoining pages. They may have been prepared in order to regulate the management and development of an estate, perhaps preparatory to selling it, or alternatively because all or a part of it had recently been purchased. Some were produced specifically to illustrate a proposed or recently completed development for housing or industrial purposes. The amount of detail provided varied a great deal and was related both to the purpose for which a survey was made and the scale at which it was executed. If the scale permitted, it was customary to show the plots into which urban property was subdivided and their dimensions and area as well. It became increasingly common for a plan of the premises to be included with the deeds of transfer on the sale of a property. This was fairly common by the nineteenth century, perhaps with an outline plan of the internal arrangements of the ground floor of the buildings. This represents fragmentary evidence, but may be useful nevertheless, especially if the premises depicted were typical of others in a group or terrace.

Many such plans carry the names of the owners of the adjoining properties and specify the nature of the boundaries, indicating if they are brick walls, for example. Some plans were executed specifically to provide evidence in a legal case relating to the land or the rights of way across it. This applied both to individual parcels of land and to the jurisdiction over larger areas. A late sixteenth-century plan of the cathedral close at Exeter related to disputes between the dean and chapter and the city corporation, and there may have been a similar reason for the preparation of a plan of St Sidwell's fee, beyond the city's East Gate, which also belonged to the dean and chapter, dating.from *c.* 1600.[13] A frequent cause of disputes in the parliamentary boroughs concerned voting rights, and their investigation sometimes prompted the preparation of plans showing the extent of the burgage plots which carried the right to vote. The electoral geography of such towns was investigated as part of the reform movement of the 1830s and was illustrated by a set of plans at one and two inches to the mile, produced in 1832, and by a further set at four inches to the mile which accompanied the *Report of the Municipal Corporation Boundaries Commission,* five years later.[14]

## Deposited plans

The details of property ownership had to be investigated when the construction of new lines of communication and public utilities was being considered. The turnpike trusts, canal, railway, tram and omnibus companies produced numerous plans illustrating their intended schemes. Proposed undertakings such as docks and gas works also required the preparation of explanatory plans. Because of public interest, some of these were printed, but a far greater number exists in manuscript. Their value lies in their detailed coverage of those parts of a town which would be affected by the development. Because of the amount of detail required, urban areas were often shown on a large-scale inset to the plans of intended road, canal or railway routes. The 'deposited plans' – compulsory after 1792 – are particularly useful, for they were the basis for the authorizing legislation, and so were accurately surveyed and have accompanying books of reference itemizing the properties affected. They are to be found amongst quarter sessions records and in the House of Lords record office. Those issued when a scheme was first proposed are rather less reliable and may be located in the appropriate local record office and in a fairly large collection in the British Library.

Deposited plans and explanatory books of reference were also produced when open field and common land were enclosed by an Act of Parliament, a device which was widely employed during the period from the second quarter of the eighteenth century until the middle of the nineteenth. Obviously, the primary purpose of the maps did not relate to urban land, but towns were sometimes surveyed and included on the plan of the area affected by the enclosure. The amount of detail provided within the urban area may not be very great, yet enclosure plans can give a valuable delineation of a town for a period before the systematic production of large-scale maps. Similarly, the maps which were produced as a result of the Tithe Commutation Act of 1836, also concerned primarily with agricultural land, cover urban areas as well, because almost all towns contained garden plots or parcels of farm land which were tithable. In some cases the urban land is included on large-scale insets to the main plans. The plans and the accompanying schedules provide evidence for the limits of building, property ownership and estate boundaries, although the areas not subject to tithes may be shown only in outline.

## The Ordnance Survey's town plans

Many of the plans described so far were produced for a specific purpose or to show a particular feature, and the area covered and the scale adopted were governed by the nature of the plan. The beginning of the Ordnance Survey's large scale coverage of towns was prompted by a growing concern about public health, stimulated by the cholera epidemics of the 1830s and 1840s. It was recognized that the necessary improvements in sanitation could only be achieved if urban areas were adequately mapped. The Ordnance Survey prepared a number of plans for the Boards of Health in the early 1850s. As they were to be used in planning and constructing proper sewerage and drainage systems and a satisfactory water supply, in accordance with the recommendations of the General Board of Health, they carry appropriate detail, such as numerous spot heights, so that sufficient falls were achieved.

The Ordnance Survey's town plans that were prepared from the mid-nineteenth century had no such specific objective, however. They covered an entire town at a constant scale – albeit on several sheets in the majority of cases – and were produced to rigorous standards at a time when surveying and cartographic techniques had been refined. They did not anticipate developments, but only showed features that existed at the time of the survey. Military requirements were important influences on the development of cartography, and the first mapping undertaken by the Board of Ordnance at the end of the eighteenth century was a survey of the coastal counties of Essex, Kent and Sussex, as they were the most exposed to a possible French invasion. This survey, at one inch to the mile, was later extended to cover the whole country, a process which took until almost 1870 to complete. In the 1850s large-scale mapping at 25 inches to the mile (1:2500) began and in 1862 this scale was adopted for coverage of the whole country. The six inch to the mile maps were derived from the 25-inch series and, because of the smaller scale, omit some detail in congested urban areas. The 25-inch plans were revised in the early years of this century and again between the two World Wars, so that changes can be traced at the same scale. These really fine plans show all topographical features to scale, without the distortion which is necessary at the smaller scales, representing railway lines to a scale width, rather than conventionally, for example. Virtually all buildings are shown, as are property boundaries and much information on urban land use. Many 25-inch plans of urban areas are currently being made available as reprints of the first two issues, at a scale reduced to approximately three-fifths of the original, but in a form which makes them suitable for use in the field. The

25–inch plans are probably adequate for the needs of most urban historians.

Much larger scale plans of almost 400 towns and cities were produced by the Ordnance Survey between 1855 and 1894. These were at the scale of more than ten-and-a-half *feet* to the mile (1: 500), requiring in excess of 300 sheets to cover a city the size of Liverpool. This makes them somewhat unwieldy to use if the aim is to achieve an overall picture of a large town, but that drawback is more than compensated for by the tremendous amount of detail which they carry and the degree of accuracy that could be achieved at such a large scale. The amount of detailed information on the use to which buildings were being put is, for example, correspondingly greater than on the 25–inch sheets. These plans are invaluable sources for the study of the micro-geography of late Victorian cities and towns. No further plans at this scale were issued, however, and the largest scale plans currently produced by the Ordnance Survey are those at 1: 1250, which were introduced in 1911 and carry essentially the same topographical information as those at the 25–inch scale. The arrangement followed by the Ordnance Survey in the London area was rather different. A skeletal survey had been made of the metropolitan area between 1847 and 1852 – before the decision was taken to survey towns at the 1: 500 scale – and plans were produced from it at 1: 1056, or five feet to one mile. This scale became the basis for the large-scale plans of London which were completed 1862–71 and, unlike the 1: 500 series, were later revised, in the early 1890s and again between 1906 and 1909.

These plans set new standards in urban mapping and superseded existing surveys for official purposes. They have been extensively used by the government and local authority departments, having an obvious application for various aspects of planning. The annotated working copies of such departments may be available, although without appropriate explanatory information the purpose of the additions may not always be entirely clear. They came to serve, too, as the basis for the detailed plans which, together with drawings and much other evidence, were included in the reports of the local medical officers of health, the parliamentary select committees and the Royal Commissions which were set up because of concern with public health and social conditions. This is invaluable evidence for studying the medical and social geography of Victorian and Edwardian towns and cities. To these should be added the independent surveys, most notably Charles Booth's detailed investigation of London in the late nineteenth century, which was illustrated by maps of the capital's social geography.

The Ordnance Survey's plans also provided the source for the maps and plans which commercial publishers issued in increasing numbers, in both sheet and atlas form and as illustrations in gazetteers and directories. The proliferation of such material in the nineteenth century was partly a result of changes in the methods of map production. The development of lithography greatly facilitated map publication and the process allowed colour printing; maps taken from a copper plate had to be hand finished if colour was required.

## Fire insurance plans

Plans of urban property had an obvious value for the fire insurance companies. The earliest plans compiled specifically for the purpose of plotting fire insurance liabilities were drawn up towards the end of the eighteenth century, and the Phoenix Fire Office was an important sponsor of Richard Horwood's plan of London of 1799. The first actual fire insurance plans to be published were those produced by James Loveday covering a part of central London, which appeared in 1857.[15] From the 1880s the fire insurance plan business was dominated by Charles Goad, whose initial set of 73 volumes was issued between 1885 and 1896 and includes plans of 34 of the largest cities and towns in England and Wales, almost all of them at the scale of one inch to 40 feet. As they were compiled to show the degree of fire risk of the various premises, they not only specify the function of each property but also mark such individual hazards as factory chimneys and steam boilers. They also provide information on the number of storeys in a building and the materials from which it was constructed, particularly those of the party walls and roofs. The plans concentrate on industrial, commercial and business premises and contain fine evidence for the central commercial areas of the towns and cities which have been covered, but are far less informative on housing and indeed do not cover those districts which were largely residential. They were continually revised, the practice being to treat a sheet as a palimpsest, with the new information for a site pasted over the original delineation. Complete revisions were produced from time to time and these are dated, but some sheets present the researcher with a plan which is a compilation made over a number of years and is of no certain date. Despite such difficulties, the revisions provide evidence from which to chart the changes in the buildings occupying the sites covered by the Goad surveyors. The 1885–96 set of plans is in the British Library's collections, with the later ones more widely available in local record offices and libraries.[16]

## *The Atlas of Historic Towns*

Recording and dealing with the evidence provided by town plans may present some problems. If a plan is consulted in order to resolve particular questions, then descriptive notes may suffice, but there are likely to be difficulties in comparing a number of plans of an area which were compiled to varied standards, at different dates, for dissimilar purposes and at different scales. The solution adopted in *The Atlas of Historic Towns*

(1969, 1975) offers a model for a topographical study based upon maps and plans. The first two volumes cover twelve cities and towns, using a standard methodology and one that is generally applicable. The *Atlas* tends to cover the entire urban area, perhaps focusing especially on the medieval core, but the technique can also be applied to individual districts, in charting the stages of suburban expansion, for example. The procedure is to select a base map as a standard and to transfer the information from the various available plans onto it, using fixed points, such as churches and bridges, to do so.

For the *Atlas* a map of *c.* 1800 is chosen as the base, before the period of rapid urbanization, but the date selected will depend on the availability of an original map and the period which is being investigated. A series of plans can be produced from the chosen base, at a constant scale, and so directly comparable. The themes illustrated depend upon the object of the research. The *Atlas* usually has a map of the physical characteristics of the site, highlighting contours and spot heights – which tend to be rather difficult to identify on urban plans – another showing the late medieval features, and one carrying the parish and ward boundaries. It marks the dominant features and buildings, such as castles, and the sites of the original settlements: the Roman Segontium at Caernarvon and the Anglo-Saxon burgh at Hereford. The chapter on Bristol has a plan which illustrates the medieval water supply, with the known sites of wells and conduits picked out, and another plan shows Clifton in *c.* 1820.[17] Those aspects of a town which are shown on plans of this kind depend upon the characteristics of the community being studied, the period and subject of the research, and the other available evidence which can be used in conjunction with the cartographic material.

# Chapter Three
# BUILDINGS

The best evidence for studying the urban fabric lies in the surviving buildings themselves, but they are not always easy to interpret without reference to the records, which may provide information on the decision to build, the date and cost of construction, the names of the developer, architect and builder, and on any subsequent additions and internal rearrangements. Documentary evidence has to be relied on for the previous generations of buildings and the rate of replacement is such that there may be several such generations to be described. This is especially true of town centres, which are the longest occupied parts of towns and those which are most subject to rebuilding. Maps and plans are important sources for this kind of study, and other records relating to the ownership, management, sale and taxation of property, the construction of buildings and their insurance against loss or damage by fire can be drawn upon, as well as probate records and pictorial material.

## Deed and leases

Conveyances of ownership and other transactions involving property are recorded in documents known collectively as deeds. This generic term covers a range of documents in different forms. The feoffment was a relic of feudal law, the operative section of the document being the endorsement recording the physical entry of the grantee into the premises. Two common forms of deed, the lease and release and the bargain and sale, were types of transfer that were devised rather later, in response to the Statute of Uses of 1535, which was not repealed until 1845. Conveyancing was also effected by means of fictitious suits by which the vendor was sued by the buyer for possession, with agreement, recorded in a final concord, being reached before judgement was given. This practice continued for more than six centuries, until its abolition in 1833. One copy of the deed produced by this method remained with the Court of Common Pleas, where the action was brought, and was entered on the Feet of Fines, which are retained in class CP 25 in the Public Record Office, Chancery Lane. The common recovery was also a fictitious suit in Common Pleas, by which the grantee, or recoverer, was awarded possession of the property by a judgement of the court. Transfers of property held by copyhold tenure were recorded in the manorial courts.

They can be traced in the court rolls and the occasional surveys, which provide the names of the holders of property within the manor and perhaps some incidental information on the premises. The copyholder's title deed was a copy of the entry in the court roll. Copyhold tenure was abolished by the Law of Property Act of 1922.

One of the problems relating to the use of deeds is assessing their representativeness, for their survival has been erratic. Deeds pass with the property to which they relate, but since 1925 evidence of title has had to be proved only for the preceding 50 years and so it has not been necessary to retain earlier documents. Many deeds were probably despatched in response to the appeal for salvage in the Second World War and some have been discovered wedged behind panelling, suggesting that their suitability as draught excluders may have led to other losses. Nevertheless, deeds do exist in large quantities, especially in family papers and solicitors' collections, many of which have been deposited in record offices. It was not unusual for property owners to entrust their deeds to their bank and if they subsequently failed to reclaim them, and many did fail, then the deeds remain among the bank's papers or those of its successor. Another source is the Chancery Proceedings, which contain extensive extracts from deeds which were cited as evidence in cases relating to property and buildings which came before that court. Other deeds are still in private custody, but the property in a town or district is commonly in a good many hands and, even if all of the owners can be traced, the response to requests to consult the deeds is likely to be disappointing. Indeed, the available deeds may not relate to all of the properties in the area being studied, or even to a representative cross-section of them. Added to the low chances of survival is the further problem that property is conveyed at irregular intervals, and long periods may occur between transfers of ownership, during which no deeds are compiled.

Enrolments of deeds are more accessible and they may provide copies of documents for properties for which the individual deeds do not survive or are not available for consultation. Deeds registers containing virtually all such records were established, by Acts of Parliament, for Middlesex and the East and West Ridings of Yorkshire in the first decade of the eighteenth century and for the North Riding from 1736. These registers principally contain deeds of sale, mortgages, and leases and assignments for 21 years or a longer term.[1] Deeds which were enrolled before the clerks of the peace were entered in the records of the civic courts (p. 109), although they represent only a comparatively small proportion of transactions. In the course of the sixteenth century the Close Rolls (Public Record Office, Chancery Lane, C 54) came to serve as a registry of private deeds and other kinds of proceedings and this practice continued until 1903.

A study based upon deeds is made easier if the land was part of an estate when it was developed, for the copies of the title documents form a coherent collection, and their survival rate has been greater than for those of property in fragmented ownership. The deeds of a corporation's property and of those charitable foundations which it administered are to be found amongst its records. They form a substantial collection in some towns. There are, for example, approximately 1,440 surviving deeds and leases of Leicester corporation's property, for the period 1510–1829.[2] Other collections of deeds have accumulated because of the purchase of property in particular types of site. Much town centre property is held by commercial organizations such as large retail companies, and the railway companies bought considerable numbers of urban houses for demolition before they constructed lines and built stations and goods yards within towns.

Deeds record the date and terms of the transaction, the names, addresses and statuses of the parties, descriptions of the properties concerned and perhaps their abutments. They also recite the previous changes of ownership, and so if a bundle of deeds for a property exists it is advisable to consult the most recent one first for its summary of the earlier transfers. The topographical detail mentioned in deeds varies a great deal, but typically includes a description of the premises, its boundaries and references to the adjoining properties with the names and statuses of their occupiers. Various items of useful information may also be noted, such as the reservation of the right of passage through a property to a specified building to its rear. Deeds for a particular plot can thereby provide evidence for the nearby premises. Where enough deeds survive, it should be possible to reconstruct schematically the layout, occupancy and ownership of properties in a district. One potential difficulty is that when properties were sold *en bloc* the deeds did not always contain details of the individual premises. It is rather unusual for deeds to have descriptions of the appearances or internal arrangements of buildings, although they may be alluded to, and so changes to both of these aspects could go unrecorded. Some deeds do have accompanying plans, however, and these may carry an outline of the layout of the ground floor. The uses to which buildings were being put were usually specified in deeds, or at least implied in some way. These generalizations do not apply to fines and common recoveries, which carry much less specific information than do other conveyances. Indeed, relatively little topographical evidence can be extracted from such deeds.

Leases provided for property to be held by tenants for a fixed term. Both parties to the contract received a copy of the document and it was also a common practice for landlords such as borough corporations and the church to enter transcripts of their leases in volumes, which may be indexed. Leases are of a fairly standard form, headed by the date of the agreement and the names of the lessor and lessee. The latter may not necessarily have been the occupier of the premises, who may also be named, together with a trade or status, which suggests the use to which the property was being put, if indeed that is not explicitly stated. The location of the premises may be given only in general terms, specifying no more than the parish, but some leases are much more specific and from the late eighteenth century they are usually precise. The dimensions of the ground and its abutments and a general description of the buildings are commonly included and the building materials may be mentioned. Leases from the early nineteenth century onwards are normally fairly detailed in this respect. An inventory of the contents of the building at the beginning of the term may be appended to the lease, providing a list of the rooms and an indication of their use. The fine taken by the lessor at the granting of the lease, the length of the term and the rent payable are commonly given. Leases also contain a number of covenants. Some of them are fairly standard, such as those which direct the lessee not to sublet the premises or change the use to which they were being put without the lessor's consent, and allowed the lessor the right to repossess the property if the rent was unpaid or the covenants were not adhered to. Others may be quite specific, perhaps enjoining the lessee to rebuild the premises, replace the roof, or to erect a stable or other ancillary building. Such changes normally had to be executed within a specified period and often the lessee was granted a new lease when they had been carried out, effectively extending the term of the original lease and incidentally allowing the alteration to be dated. An examination of such covenants can provide a general impression of changes in construction, such as the widespread introduction of chimneys, the replacement of thatch with tile and of timber framing with brick. Such covenants became more numerous and detailed from about the late sixteenth century onwards, with the development of the so-called 'repairing lease', by which lessors placed a greater onus for the repair and maintenance of properties on lessees. On the other hand, rents were raised little, if at all, despite inflation, and lessors received most income from the fine payable at the renewal of a lease.

## Surveys and rentals

Surveys of property commonly summarize the type of information that is available in leases. Typically, they note the condition of the property, the rents currently levied and the level to which they could be raised, the name and perhaps the occupation or status of the tenants and a valuation of the premises. Surveys and their accompanying plans are especially useful in providing a picture of an estate at a particular date. They may have been added to and altered over a number of years, thereby supplying evidence of changes of tenants, land use and property values, although the successive additions and corrections to details of this kind may be difficult to date and perhaps make the information rather confusing. Some surveys may have become separated from the relevant plans and others were produced without a plan being executed to illustrate them. While it may be more difficult to locate properties described in a survey which lacks a related plan, there may be no other deficiency in the information included.

Many surveys were compiled because an estate was to be sold. An especial case which should be mentioned is that of the so-called Parliamentary Surveys. In the seventeenth century the lands of the crown and the church were disposed of following the Civil Wars. They were surveyed and valued, prior to sale, between 1647 and 1653. Much urban property was involved; the survey of the lands of the dean of St Paul's included 700 houses at Shadwell in east London, for example.[3] These detailed surveys are a valuable source, for they contain information on the tenurial arrangements, rentals and value of the properties, as well as on their construction, dimensions, internal arrangements and the use to which they were being put. The surveys also have general observations on the tenure and customs of the manors of which the individual properties were a part. They are useful for the evidence which they provide on the condition of the buildings in the immediate aftermath of the Civil Wars, ranging from the neglected and perhaps damaged episcopal palaces and deaneries to the smaller houses and ancillary buildings. The bishop of Gloucester's palace was described as 'very ruinous and not habitable' and a tenement in the Eastgate at Lincoln, ruined during the conflict, was being rebuilt with 'rough stone', but was incomplete when it was surveyed in January 1650.[4] The surveys of the crown lands are in the Public Record Office, those of the bishops and of the capitular lands are in Lambeth Palace Library or the appropriate diocesan archives. Copies may survive amongst local records. These lands were repossessed at the Restoration and were generally granted out on new leases, many of them to their former purchasers.

Property belonging to royalist sympathizers was assessed for fines or confiscations, but it was not surveyed in such detail as were the crown and church lands. The two parliamentary committees which dealt with this aspect were those for Compounding and the Advance of Money, and their papers are calendared. Not all of the property included in this material is individually noted in the calendars, however, and although the places of residence of those being investigated are given, it is advisable to search the papers relating to all of the royalists known to have held property in a town (Public Record Office, Chancery Lane, SP 23, SP 19).

Surveys and leases contain much information on the rents payable, and a systematic record of their collection may survive in rentals. Rentals are chiefly useful as financial records and contain less evidence on properties than do the surveys and leases to which they relate. They may note the contents of the current lease, but if a property is not described it can be identified in a rental by the lessee's name and the rent payable. Rents were normally due on two, or perhaps on all four, of the quarter days. Rentals can provide evidence of economic well-being by the extent to which rents were paid on time or became overdue, both in terms of individual tenants and of a district where a landlord owned a high proportion of the premises. Researchers should beware, however, of the possible fossilization of this kind of record, with the entries copied from one collection to another, regardless of changes, and with the rent payable entered, whether or not it had been received in full.

## Sale advertisements and prospectuses

Intending vendors and lessors of property have, for the past 300 years, advertised in newspapers and magazines. Such advertisements include the estates of bankrupts. Newspapers first appeared in the mid-seventeenth century and the earliest provincial ones began to appear early in the following century; the number of titles increased rapidly after *c.* 1750. There were comparatively few advertisements for property in the early years of provincial newspapers, but they appeared in increasing numbers and had become a common feature by the end of the eighteenth century. They carry information which is not dissimilar in its nature from that in their modern counterparts. They may give a fairly precise location and usually itemize the rooms and ancillary buildings of the property, perhaps describing the building materials as well, if only in general terms. Similar information is given for industrial and service premises. The nature of present day property advertisements may lead researchers to regard such material with some slight caution, but the more strictly factual content of their precursors is somewhat reassuring. A house in the Foregate Street in Worcester, which was advertised to be let in 1743, was of brick, with sashed windows, five rooms on each floor, with a laundry, a brewhouse, stabling for six horses, a flower garden and a kitchen garden 'planted with the best Kind of Fruit'. The advertiser could not resist adding a slight flourish: 'N.B. Very few Houses have so many Conveniences.'[5] The national titles also carry such advertisements, with a bias towards premises in London and south-eastern England. A search in them for properties in a particular town is likely to be much more prolonged and rather less productive than one in the local newspapers. Such advertisements do provide an unrepresentative sample, as a great deal of urban property was not sold or leased in this way and only the more valuable and substantial premises appear in them. The most comprehensive newspaper collection is held by the British Library, but most libraries and record offices usually have good holdings of local titles.

Sale particulars contain similar information to property advertisements in newspapers and have been produced in large numbers in the nineteenth and twentieth centuries. They are generally to be found in family, estate and solicitors' collections. Proposals for new developments were also issued, in order to arouse the interest of potential buyers and to discover if the market was strong enough for the scheme to proceed. For many of the speculative schemes characteristic of the Georgian era the developer, who may also have been the builder, issued a plan and prospectus outlining the proposals and giving details of the buildings which were to be erected. When the Exeter builder Robert Stribling planned to construct Bedford Circus in the city in the early 1770s he produced a 'Description of the Manner of Building the houses of the Intended Circus at Exeter', providing details of their size and proportions and also of the materials which were to be used, and stressing the precautions taken against the spread of fire.[6] The builders of the Victorian villas which are so much a part of English townscapes also issued plans and illustrations of their projects, and indeed the practice is still followed. After the Sanitary Acts of 1875 builders were obliged to deposit such plans with the local authority and these may also have had elevations of the proposed buildings. Similar information is carried in the specialist architectural journals, the first of which was *The Builder*, which began publication in 1842, and was soon followed by a number of others, including *Building News*, from 1857, with *The Architectural Review* starting life rather later, in 1896. Some caution is necessary when using such material, however, for the proposals may have been changed before they were executed and some schemes may not have matured at all.

Property that was to be auctioned was commonly advertised in newspapers, but auctions also generated other, specialist, publications. Records of property sold at auction can be found in the *Estates Gazette* and the *Property Market Review*, which began publication in 1857 and 1893 respectively. In 1892 the *Land and House Property Year Book* was established and it continued until 1921, reappearing after an interval of a year as the *Estates Exchange Year Book*. Property in it is categorized by place; the address of the premises is given, together with the price and the date of the sale. The nature of the property is described in broad terms and the dimensions of the plot are also noted.

## Building contracts

The records of the actual construction of a building may not survive and the evidence for its date may be only an entry in a rate book, or perhaps in a deed or lease on its subsequent transfer. Builders' papers, such as accounts and correspondence, provide more precise evidence, as do the contracts which were concluded with one or more craftsmen, specifying the building or reconstruction work that was required. Some agreements of this kind were made with one man, who may himself have then contracted with others, such as carpenters and joiners, to do parts of the work. Others were contracted directly with such specialists, so that a number of such arrangements were made for the construction of a building. The contracts typically give detailed instructions, stipulating the materials to be used, the dimensions of the various features, the timetable to be followed and the price paid for the work, with the stages at which the various instalments were to be advanced. A document of this kind of 1734 provided for the erection of two pairs of houses in Banbury, one pair to be of two-and-a-half storeys with stone slated roofs, and the other, more modest, pair, to the rear of the first, of one-and-a-half storeys and thatched. The detailed contract specifies the materials to be used, including the re-use of old ones, and stipulates the incorporation of some existing walls into the new houses. The original layout of these houses has been recovered from the information given in the contract and the builder's plan. A similar document of 1701 provides for the reconstruction of a house in Gloucester and gives detailed particulars of the various features of the structure and their dimensions.[7] Such contracts are mostly to be found in family and solicitors' records. Disputes arose over the execution of some contracts of this kind and, if the case came into one of the equity courts, the contents of the agreement may exist in the form of a fairly full summary in its records (p. 125).

## Public buildings

Public buildings form a prominent part of the townscape, especially in town centres, and the sources relating to their erection should have been better preserved and be in more accessible collections than those for housing or industrial premises. A plan of Nottingham in 1820 shows the 4 parish churches, 17 chapels, 10 day and sunday schools, 15 almshouses and hospitals, 3 workhouses, the lunatic asylum, house of correction, assembly rooms, theatre, library and newsroom, post office, shambles and, as it was a county town, a town hall and a county hall, both incorporating gaols.[8] A port would also have a customs house and, as the nineteenth century progressed, at least one railway station was constructed in virtually every town, as well as gasworks, waterworks and power stations, museums and art galleries, concert halls, colleges and universities, baths and washhouses. The number of buildings directly under public control increased considerably after the mid-nineteenth century as the civic authorities became responsible for education, health, welfare and housing. The same period also saw an increase in the numbers of churches and chapels built – 15 were erected in Oldham between 1870 and 1888, for example[9] – as well as of offices, shops and banks, which came to form the dominant elements in most town centres.

Information on the construction of the churches and chapels is to be found in the parochial, diocesan and appropriate denominational records. A major source for the anglican churches is the diocesan faculty papers, which include those faculties which were granted for the erection and structural alterations of church buildings. The records of the Commissioners for Building New Churches under the Act of Parliament of 1818, which sought to tackle the problem of under-provision of churches in the expanding urban areas, are in the custody of the Church Commissioners, and a list of the churches that were erected with some assistance from Parliamentary grants between 1818 and 1856 is included in M.H. Port, *Six Hundred New Churches* (1961). An important source for the period 1862 to 1916 is provided by *The Church Builder*, a quarterly, which contains lists of both new and enlarged churches, with such details as the date of consecration, the style and chief features of the building and the name of the architect. New mission halls, chapels and church schools are also listed. The architectural press, such as *The Builder*, also has fairly good coverage of new churches and chapels.

Details of the construction of the buildings of public utilities are amongst the papers of the relevant companies. The bulk of the railway companies' records are deposited at the Public Record Office at Kew, but others may be retained by the British Rail property board or in its regional offices. The papers of the gas companies are generally to be found in local record offices or with those of the successor organizations which took over from them. These were the relevant local urban authorities in many cases. For the buildings belonging to or administered by the corporations there is generally a great deal of information in their records, for they were an important element in civic identity. Town halls, in particular, were both symbolic and functional: visible manifestations of civic independence and the point from which urban administration was directed. Hence the two periods when many towns first obtained a charter – the years after the Reformation and those following the Municipal Corporations Act of 1835 – were also those during which many town halls were built. For the earlier periods a borough's administrative records may contain the decision to build and the specifications of a new town hall, perhaps even the accounts for its construction. With the transition from vernacular building styles to those which were designed by architects of regional or national importance, the scale and costs of the buildings both increased, culminating in the great nineteenth-century town halls, such as those at Birmingham, built in the 1830s, and Leeds, which cost £122,000 in the 1850s.[10] These and other public buildings of the nineteenth and twentieth centuries are much more fully documented than are their predecessors. There may be detailed plans and also correspondence, notes of the tenders submitted for the work, accounts for construction and fitting, and minutes of the committees overseeing their erection. Their progress from conception to completion can also generally be traced in the local press. The survival of similar material relating to the construction of factories, shops, banks and other commercial premises has been more erratic, partly because of the relatively short life of companies, many of which were liquidated or absorbed by others. Commercial premises also appear on many illustrated company bill heads and in their advertisements. Business papers may be amongst those of the successor companies, deposited in local record offices, or may have found their way into the Public Record Office's holdings as exhibits in court cases. Some architects' models have survived and those that have tend to be kept within the buildings to which they relate. They provide a three-dimensional picture of a structure as it was planned, before any subsequent alterations, additions or reconstruction.

## Building Acts and district surveyors' returns

That the styles and appearance of buildings vary from one period to another is largely a reflection of changing tastes, but they have also been influenced by the building controls imposed through both national legislation and local authority by-laws during the eighteenth and nineteenth centuries, which placed certain restrictions upon design and construction. The measures taken in London to control rebuilding after the Great Fire were subsequently developed and added to and were very influential, being drawn upon by provincial cities and towns for their own regulations. The impact of such controls upon the alignment, scale and appearance of houses was such that they gave rise to a style which is referred to as 'by-law housing'. The details of the controls varied from town to town, although they had much in common and indeed Victorian governments sought to bring about some standardization through such measures as the Public Health Act of 1875 and the Model By-Laws of 1877.[11]

Fire controls in London were set out in a succession of Building Acts, with those of 1763 and 1774 being especially important. They divided buildings into seven categories or 'classes' and stipulated that newly erected and altered houses had to be examined by a surveyor, who certified in an affidavit that the work conformed to the terms of the Acts. The affidavits contain the names of the builders and the position of the houses, and the certificates returned on the condition and placing of party walls give the names of the owners or occupiers of the properties concerned. This information is also contained in several volumes of registers. The 1774 Act was superseded by the Metropolitan Building Act of 1844. By the terms of this measure the district surveyors made monthly returns, upon printed forms, of works executed under their supervision. Buildings were categorized in three broad groups: dwelling houses; warehouses, factories and similar structures; and public buildings. All new buildings and rebuildings were included as well as alterations such as the insertion of new shop fronts and the reconstruction of chimney stacks. The returns made following the 1855 Building Act include some indication of the height of the structure and perhaps mention the number of storeys.[12] The chronology of building construction can be tabulated from such returns. Moreover, from the notices of dangerous structures there is evidence of the physical condition of existing buildings, and a plot of their distribution indicates streets or districts in which properties were in a generally dilapidated state. The information which the returns supply on the builders who were active in a locality, and on property ownership, can also be valuable.

## Fire insurance policies

The Great Fire of London was also an important stimulus to the development of the fire insurance business, which generated a category of records that is especially useful for the study of buildings. The policies which were issued by the fire insurance companies describe, in broad terms, the insured properties and may also mention their contents. Individual policies are to be found amongst family papers and in solicitors' collections. The records of the local agents engaged by the companies may be deposited in local record offices, but they typically cover a particular area and for only a relatively short period. The policies are most accessible through the registers of the insurance companies, which may be in the hands of the companies or their successors, in local record offices, or in the Guildhall Library's collections. The registers of the Hand-in-Hand begin in 1696 and are the earliest such records – its business was confined mainly to London, during the eighteenth century at least – and those of the Sun Fire Office, which cover its much more widespread operations, commence in 1710. Both sets of registers are in the Guildhall Library. Policy registers are commonly unindexed and locating policies for a particular town, district or property can be time consuming and somewhat frustrating. They do have extenuating features in this respect, however. Firstly, agents returned policies periodically in batches and so those for a town or area are to be found grouped roughly together in the registers. Secondly, for tracing an individual property, the duration of a policy provides an indication of when the next one would be issued and so this can be found relatively quickly, for the policies are normally arranged in a chronological sequence.

Housing, service buildings (such as inns) and industrial premises are all included within this source. The policies typically give the name of the owner of the property, that of the occupier – with an occupation or status – and the purpose to which the building was being put, itemizing ancillary structures as well. Those of the Hand-in-Hand also give the dimensions of buildings. The essential information which the insurance companies required was the degree of fire risk that the premises represented, so policies commonly mention the building and roofing materials and perhaps describe the nature of the neighbouring properties. In 1728 the Sun issued a policy to Humphrey Ray, gentleman, for two brick houses in West Street, Gravesend, both of which were covered with slate or tile and had adjoining timber built offices. The houses were occupied by Captain William Parker and William Man, gentleman, and were insured for £200 and £250 respectively; the former also had a timber summer house at the end of the garden which was insured for £50. The same company's policy for the premises of a London silver-smith in 1802 gives the address of the house and refers to the kitchen, with the counting house over it, a range of workshops and a 'Steam Engine House' to the rear of the counting house, and further workshops on the north side of the yard. The contents were insured in a separate policy.[13]

Fire insurance policies are a fine source for a study of the built environment. They are particularly useful for the evidence which they provide on the construction and layout of factories and workshops. Commercial establishments are well represented in the policies; all but 12 of Nottingham's 68 hosiery firms in 1771 had their premises insured with the Sun, for example.[14] The valuations should be fairly realistic ones – although there may be some doubt whether they were kept entirely up-to-date during periods of inflation – and they can be used to trace changes in property values. Descriptions of roofing materials in the policies can indicate the effectiveness of attempts to reduce the risks of large-scale fires. Exeter's policy of banning thatched roofs within the city walls, although not in the suburbs, is illustrated by an examination of the Sun's early eighteenth-century registers, which describe much thatched property in the extra-mural parishes but none in the prohibited area.[15]

The policies do have some drawbacks as a source. One is that not all property owners insured their premises, especially in the early days of fire insurance, and so the policies are unrepresentative, with a bias towards the buildings held by the wealthier proprietors. Nor should it be assumed that a policy includes all of the buildings in a group on a particular site, for some may have been excluded. Some premises were not insured because the companies regarded them as high risks. As early as 1727 the Sun resolved not to insure adjoining thatched premises.[16] This may mean that those towns which still had a high proportion of thatched buildings in the eighteenth century are under-represented. The companies constantly sought to minimize their liabilities, both in terms of such general exclusions and in specific cases which the company's inspecting surveyor regarded as unsatisfactory. Decisions of this kind and the response to claims made after fires can be found amongst the companies' minutes and in their letter books.

## Probate inventories

Probate inventories provide much information on the contents and perhaps the internal arrangements of buildings, although they rarely mention the nature of the fabric. They are lists of the personal estates of deceased persons and survive in large numbers for most regions from the mid sixteenth until the late eighteenth centuries (pp. 63–5). The appraisers who undertook the task of compiling an inventory generally itemized the deceased's effects room by room, describing the function of the rooms and ancillary buildings as they did so. If the nature of the rooms and buildings is not specified, their purpose can usually be inferred from their contents.

The appraisers of the estate of William Allen of Sittingbourne, a surgeon, who died in 1725, listed his goods in the kitchen, buttery, parlour, washhouse, best chamber, other chambers, cellar and 'Physick Room', which contained drugs, medicines, bottles, instruments and books.[17] The inventory of Jeffery Atterbury was compiled in 1734 and lists his belongings in his house at Kensington, room by room. The two garrets were both used as bedrooms and the passage between them also contained a bed. The fore and the back chambers were both bedrooms, but were more comfortably furnished than the garrets, especially the one at the front of the house, which had decorations that included a picture and six prints and also contained some Delft ware. The remaining rooms were a parlour, kitchen, buttery and a 'back room over the cellar', while the cellars themselves were put to a sensible use, containing 36 barrels of beer and two gallons of brandy. It is likely that the buttery stood apart from the house, adjoining the yard, which is also mentioned in the inventory. The goods are valued by room and the contrast between, for instance, the comparatively sparsely furnished back garret, the contents of which were estimated to be worth £1 15s. 6d., and the front chamber, with furnishings and other goods valued at £8 3s. 6d., is indicative of their relative size and the use to which they were put. A feature of this particular inventory is that it also has a note on the title of Atterbury's two tenements, one of which is the house described in the document.[18]

One difficulty of using probate inventories to reconstruct the layout of a house is that some rooms may have been empty, or they contained goods which either did not belong to the deceased or were of such low value that they were not listed. In such cases the researcher is unknowingly presented with an incomplete record. With this proviso in mind, where a probate inventory can be successfully related to a surviving building – itself a difficult task – it should be possible to correlate the contents of the document with the various rooms. Analysis of the numbers and usage of rooms and the values of the goods provides an insight into the relative prosperity of the different categories within the urban population, not including the poor, and perhaps the localization of occupations in the town. A study of the probate inventories for Norwich has shown that the use of attics for working purposes, chiefly weaving, was not common in the city before the 1680s.[9] Many wills also contain descriptions of bequeathed property and goods, but these items are noted in a less systematic manner than in the inventories and the items mentioned can rarely, if ever, have been a complete list of the testator's possessions.

## Taxation and rating

The majority of early-modern taxation records provide little information on urban topography, being chiefly lists of taxpayers and the sums at which they were assessed. The returns of the Hearth Tax, which was levied between 1662 and 1689, are an exception, for they show the numbers of hearths for each householder and some of them also contain that information for those householders poor enough to be exempt from the tax (p. 59). The owners of empty properties were also liable to pay the tax. While households should not necessarily be equated with houses, this data can be used to give some indication of relative property sizes. It may be possible, for example, to identify the councillors in the returns and compare the size of their properties, in terms of hearths, with the average for the community, and perhaps plot their distribution. The way in which the entries are listed makes it difficult to tie many of the returns to the topography of a town in any detailed way, however, for street names are rarely given and the ward is commonly the smallest unit that can be identified. While the larger buildings, such as inns, may be recognized, seldom is it possible to trace changes of occupancy between assessments with any confidence, for the majority of properties.

Examination of a series of comparable taxation returns can give an indication of changes in the relative sizes of the parishes or wards between collections. Leases, surveys and rentals are much more precise sources for tracing new buildings and from them the development of a district can be followed in some detail, but they are not available for all areas. The value of commercial directories in this respect is limited to the central business areas of towns, where their coverage was reasonably good, but even so they do not provide complete lists of householders and many streets are omitted from them. A series of plans can also be employed, but because of irregular revisions they supply only intermittent evidence. The decennial census returns from 1841 provide a regular sequence which can be used for the purpose, although they cannot give precise dating of the developments between the census years and have the further drawback that they are closed to the public for 100 years.

Ratebooks were compiled more frequently than these sources and they may cover a long period, in some parishes from the sixteenth century, although an unbroken series normally begins much later. The use of books designed and printed for the purpose became fairly common in the late eighteenth century and that seems to have increased their chances of survival. They consist of lists of occupiers from whom rates were levied on an annual, or perhaps more frequent, basis and the sums payable. Some contain terse annotations regarding the demolition or rebuilding of properties. The normal and indeed logical form was for the collectors to list the names of the ratepayers in order of property, so that the ratebooks can be used to follow their progress along a street. It may be that corner houses were not entered in the same street at all collections, however, and the collectors may have varied their route occasionally. It is advisable to use the more recent ratebooks first, for identification of property is a relatively easy task in those books which were compiled when houses had been numbered, care always being taken over possible renumbering, and a scheme drawn up from that evidence can serve as a fairly secure basis upon which to study the earlier lists. Comparison of a series of lists reveals changes of names amongst the ratepayers and insertions and additions, which may indicate new housing, factories and warehouses, or subdivision of the existing properties. They are most difficult to interpret accurately for the early stages of a new street or development, when there were still gaps between the houses in an incomplete group and the collectors had not arranged their route in a settled and ordered house-to-house perambulation. Nevertheless, it should be possible to date and piece together the pattern of new constructions from the evidence of ratebooks, but with the further proviso that the poorest householders, who were exempt from paying the rates, do not appear in the books.

Some vestries carried out comprehensive surveys of property for rating purposes, often because of new developments in a parish. Many of these were undertaken in the years immediately following the 1836 Act to Regulate Parochial Assessments, which brought uniformity to the rating system, and consisted of plans and accompanying schedules.[20] Their survival has not been good, but where such a survey does exist it provides a point to which the evidence of the ratebooks can be anchored.

Changes in property ownership and the subdivision of plots for building can also be traced from the annual or more frequent Land Tax returns. The tax was introduced in 1692. Survival of returns from before 1780 has been patchy, but from that date until 1832 they had to be lodged with the clerk of the peace to establish voters' qualifications. They list the names of the owners and occupiers of taxable land and the sums payable. A great deal of urban property did not have such land attached and so went unrecorded in the returns, a feature which was obviously greater in the larger towns and cities than in country towns. The extent of such unassessed property makes the Land Tax returns an altogether more difficult and less rewarding source for urban historians than ratebooks.

In addition to property valuations for local authority rating purposes, a comprehensive and national assessment is provided by the Valuation Office records. A valuation of property was required in order to implement the terms of the 1909/10 Finance Act which related to the new increment value duty. Reassessments were made until the duty was abolished by the 1920 Finance Act. Valuation districts and sub-districts were created and each property was given an identity, known as an hereditament number. These numbers and the boundaries of the districts and sub-districts were added to Ordnance Survey base plans. Two series of plans were produced; the working plans may be in the local record offices and the record copies are in the Public Record Office at Kew. The latter have to be used to locate properties in the volumes of Valuers' Field Books, also at Kew (IR 58). The volumes contain the names and addresses of owners, details of tenancies and sub-tenancies and generally an indication of the liability for repairs and payment of rates and insurance. The type of property is usually noted in a brief description and the area which it covered is shown. An indication of the age of a building is given, but only in vague terms, such as 'old' or 'fairly modern', although building work after 1909 can be dated fairly precisely. The number of rooms in a building and its condition are described in varying, but usually good, detail. A picture of the state of particular streets and localities can be formed from this source and notes may also have been added by the valuers indicating their general impression of the type of society which they found there, such as 'A rough street'. Such particulars and comments are not included in the second series of volumes created under the 1909/10 Act and known as the 'Domesday Books'. They were offered to the local record offices in 1979 and were generally accepted. They give the names of the owners and occupiers and gross and rateable values, but are much less informative than are the Field Books.

## Pictorial and archaeological evidence

The illustrations which many cartographers placed around the perimeters of town plans were commonly perspective views of the town and elevations of the principal public buildings, churches and the houses of the urban elite. They represent only the tip of the iceberg of illustrative material available to urban historians. Large numbers of drawings, sketches, prints, engravings and paintings also survive, showing individual buildings – both public and private – streets, courts and alleys, town centres, as well as panoramas of entire districts or towns. Some of this material was published in local histories, directories and guide books, but the vast majority of it remains unpublished and can be traced in local catalogues and with the help of M.W. Barley's A Guide to British Topographical Collections (1974).

The earliest illustrations of urban topography date from the late sixteenth century and for the next hundred years or so foreign artists and engravers, such as the prolific Wenceslaus Hollar, were dominant in the production of English urban scenes. During the Stuart period London, Oxford and Cambridge were especially well covered. The best known eighteenth century material is that of Samuel and Nathaniel Buck, who produced 89 different urban views, and William Stukeley, while the versatile Joseph Farington's *Views of Cities and Towns in England and Wales* (1790) was devoted to urban scenes. For the late eighteenth and early nineteenth centuries the drawings of J. and J.C. Buckler constitute a large and valuable collection, most of which is in the British Library, with a part of it in the Bodleian Library. Architectural drawings were produced in increasing numbers in the nineteenth century and there are numerous illustrations in specialist journals and other publications which covered architectural matters. These can be taken to be accurate reproductions of the buildings and scenes portrayed. The work of artists in oils, sketches and water-colours is generally relatively straightforward and can be used to provide topographical evidence, although it may be derivative or have been intended to illustrate a scene retrospectively, creating problems of dating and accuracy.[21] Fortunately, they did not confine their work to town centres, the principal streets and the larger or conventionally attractive buildings, but also portrayed alleys and courts and scenes of urban decay. A number of drawings which John Crome made of early nineteenth-century Norwich, for example, show dilapidated buildings, providing not only evidence of economic and social conditions in the city at that time, but also architectural details of the buildings, especially of those whose interiors are revealed by collapsed external walls and roofs.[22] For the earlier periods the uneven survival of such illustrative material makes it difficult to obtain more than a general impression of the characteristic features of a town, but for the nineteenth century it should be possible to reconstruct the appearance of at least parts of the townscape with some degree of confidence.

Photographs add a further dimension to the visual evidence for studying townscapes. They survive from the mid nineteenth century and in relatively large numbers from the 1870s onwards. Most towns have fairly sizeable collections, which include postcards, and these are still expanding as a result of the increasing recognition of and interest in the historical value of such material. There are also national collections at the Public Record Office and the National Library of Wales, and the Greater London History Library has an important collection for London. The reproduction of photographs and postcards from the late Victorian and Edwardian periods has been a popular form of local history publishing in recent years. Many publications of this kind concentrate largely upon the pictorial evidence of social conditions which photographs provide. They are of equal value for the study of urban topography, showing buildings, street furniture and transport systems. It may be possible to trace successive views of sections of townscape from the mid nineteenth century, illustrating the replacement of buildings and changes in building styles and materials. They provide evidence of buildings erected considerably earlier. Indeed, it is often surprising to see the extent of the survival of seventeenth- or early eighteenth-century timber and thatch structures in late nineteenth-century town centres, particularly where none now survive because of their subsequent removal as the rate of urban building replacement quickened. The problems which most commonly occur in using photographic evidence are accurate dating, for relatively few photographs and postcards are dated – the glass negatives are almost invariably undated – and positive identification of the scene portrayed, especially if it is of one of those minor streets or alleys which lack distinctive buildings that can be used for the purpose.

The difficulties of identifying the locations recorded in photographic and documentary sources can often be overcome by fieldwork. Many topographical problems which appear rather confusing when encountered in the documents can be resolved when an area is visited. For identifying buildings and sites mentioned in the sources and plotting recent changes, there is no substitute for fieldwork. It also serves to add stylistic to documentary evidence for dating purposes, and a comparison of modern façades with those shown on early photographs of the same buildings can be an instructive exercise. The rate of development in most town centres is such that a systematic photographic survey will very soon become an illustration of modern changes in the townscape, as well as a record of earlier buildings.

Where access can be obtained, surveys should also be made of the internal arrangements of buildings, which are also subject to considerable changes. Such internal investigation of buildings often reveals interesting features concealed behind modern or mundane facades, indicating both structural alterations and changes of use, and perhaps providing important clues for dating. Reconstruction of earlier layouts is a complex and difficult task in most cases, requiring the expertise of architectural historians and urban archaeologists. Their reports are good sources of information on urban buildings and topography and with the expansion of medieval and post-medieval archaeology in recent years they are becoming available in increasing numbers in academic and local societies' journals. They contain plans, elevations and isometric drawings of standing structures and demolished buildings whose sites have been excavated, as well as much technical information concerning construction and building materials. Their evidence for the built environment can be set beside the kinds of illustrative material discussed above. Such reports also illustrate and analyse the domestic artefacts, such as pottery, recovered in excavations, which shed much light on the social conditions of the people who created and inhabited the urban environment.

# Chapter Four
# PRE-MODERN POPULATION AND SOCIETY

The sources which can be drawn upon for information for the study of urban population in the pre-modern period divide into three basic kinds. Firstly, there were enumerations which were designed to establish the size of a population, or a section of it, and a number of them can fairly be regarded as censuses. Secondly, other sources, such as taxation returns, were generated for a variety of other purposes, but can also be utilized in studying urban demography. From both of these types of source, the size, dynamics and characteristics of a town's population and its social and occupational structure can be investigated. Thirdly, there are records which contain further information on these aspects of the urban community, as well as insights into the lives and possessions of individuals, but do not provide secure evidence of a numerical kind.

A problem which can be encountered when attempting to assess the size and character of a pre-modern town is its suburbs, for the built-up area may have extended into parishes beyond the town's boundaries, yet constituted only parts of those parishes. The sources produced by the civic authorities do not cover such suburbs and others, which do include them, may not be easy to interpret. It may, for example, be difficult to assign population figures to that part of a larger parish which was occupied by a suburb. Yet to omit the suburbs would be to give a misleading impression, not only of the size of the town, but also of its social composition. Suburbs typically contained a large proportion of ale-houses, insalubrious trades, the houses and workshops of those who were not free to trade within the boundaries of the town and others who wished to avoid the scrutiny and regulations of the civic magistrates. They gradually changed in character, becoming, indeed, respectable neighbourhoods and by the early nineteenth century, in most towns, they were generally of a different nature from the typical suburbs of two or three centuries earlier.

A further difficulty in using the statistics derived from sources for the pre-modern town is that they were generated by a society which was not accustomed to the same degree of numerical exactitude as our own. The clergy, parochial officers or others whose task it was to compile the lists which we now employ were almost certainly less than fully numerate and may not have found it easy to translate their returns into the categories required. They were also likely to commit basic arithmetical errors. The standard of numeracy apparently increased considerably during the early-modern period and so the problem does diminish somewhat.[1] Moreover, by the late seventeenth century an awareness of the potential value of population statistics had begun to develop. The political economists – John Graunt, Sir William Petty and Gregory King – were collecting and analysing such data and it is apparent that some of the eighteenth-century antiquarians were also keen to gather meaningful figures. In the nineteenth century such interest became something of a passion and the urban historian, rather than dealing with comparatively little information of dubious veracity, is more likely to be distressed by the sheer amount of statistical information available.

## Enumerations

The general enumerations of urban population made before the official censuses of the nineteenth century were taken in a whole range of towns. There are surviving ones for the relatively small towns, such as Bewdley, Tewkesbury and Guildford, as well as for the larger and expanding ones. They survive from the whole of the early modern period. There was a census of Coventry in 1523 which included the numbers of empty houses – it was a time of economic dislocation for the town – and an informative one for Poole taken in 1574.[2] They were compiled in increasing numbers from the late seventeenth century onwards. Many were the result of the antiquarians' growing interest in population matters and the results were summarized for inclusion in local or county histories or as part of the information presented on town plans. Taylor's plan of Hereford of 1757 shows, on an inset, the numbers of houses and inhabitants by street, with the figures for the almshouses given separately from those for the streets in which they stood. The variety in the density of population and the occupancy rates per house within the city can therefore be evaluated. Other enumerations were compiled to make a particular point, perhaps to support a petition for assistance. In 1631 a petition was presented to the Bishop of Worcester requesting authorization to rebuild a chapel in Worcester's northern suburb. In its support a list was compiled of the 350 inhabitants there, arranged by household, and headed 'the number of all our householders of all Sorts boathe poor and Riche by name . . . togeather with the number of their severall howshoulds and famylies'. The character of the area is indicated by the fact that only two of the inhabitants were servants but almost a half were inmates, that is, temporary lodgers and apprentices.[3] In this example the list of households is extant, but other enumerations survive only in a summarized form. This is the case with an enumeration of St Anne, Soho, which was taken in 1711 at the instance of the Commissioners for Building Fifty New Churches. It was a true census, for the parochial officers were instructed 'to goe from House to House and take the Number of the severall

Inhabitants'. The results of their investigations were presented in seven categories: English inhabitants; English children under ten; English servants; French inhabitants; French children under ten; French servants; and 'Lodgers who are chiefly French, their Children and Servants', who made up 41 per cent of the parish's population. Apart from the demographic information in this record, it is also of value for illustrating the extent of Huguenot immigration into this part of London's West End.[4]

In some instances the origin and purpose of such enumerations are not known, making their interpretation rather difficult. Nor can all enumerations be taken to be reliable guides to the size of the populations nominally included in them, for accuracy cannot be assumed. There is always the possibility that they were not made from door to door, as a census should be, but were compiled from local knowledge, perhaps by clergymen or others with access to such records as parish registers and ratebooks. Hostility to the taking of censuses remained strong, for they were popularly associated with taxation, and this may have deterred would-be enumerators, especially those who did not have official authority. The compilers of such population figures may also have succumbed to the temptation to exaggerate the numbers of inhabitants, for there was a tendency to equate size with importance and status.

Some enumerations were official returns of a part of the population for specific purposes. The muster rolls of the sixteenth and early seventeenth centuries are such a source. They were initiated in 1522 by Henry VIII's government, which had just embarked upon a war with France, in order to provide an indication of the manpower available for service in the militia. Once established, the process continued intermittently for more than a century. The rolls typically list the names of the able-bodied men over 16 years old and such weapons as they had. Some also note occupation or status, a rough indication of age and perhaps of physique. The 1608 return for Gloucestershire categorized the listed men by the weapon which they were fit to wield – pike, musket, or caliver – and those 'of the meanest stature either fit for a pyoner [sic], or of little other use'.[5] It may be that the names of those 'of little other use' were not always entered and it seems that from the mid sixteenth century it was generally thought to be inadvisable to provide military training for the lower ranks in society, who might put such training to seditious use. There may also have been some evasion, and so the completeness of the rolls varied. Indeed, some returns seem to be unreliable, especially those for the first years of Elizabeth's reign. This leads to uncertainty as to the dependability of a particular roll, and converting such lists to estimates of population size is rather hazardous without corroborative evidence. The 1608 muster for Leicester includes perhaps one-half of the men aged between 16 and 60; most of those mustered were under 40 and only 52 per cent can be identified as freemen. The names in this roll are listed by ward, and trades are given, providing the evidence for a rough occupational geography of the town. This shows that, amongst other things, 19 of the 27 tanners listed lived in a riverside ward on the fringe of the town and downstream from its central area, for sound environmental reasons. The listing of the trades suggests that some lumping into categories occurred and that some of the descriptions may be misleading. As a half of the adult males were not mustered, the picture presented may not, in any case, be a true reflection of the occupational profile of the town.[6]

The surviving Henrician rolls are noted in the *Letters and Papers, Foreign and Domestic, of the Reign of Henry VIII* and the originals are in the Augmentation Office records, Public Record Office, Chancery Lane, E 36, 101 and 315. The later ones are generally among the state papers for the reign, with survivals also in the private papers of the Lords Lieutenant of the counties, who were responsible for the militia, and in corporation archives.

Another section of the population which was occasionally counted, although for quite different reasons, was the urban poor. During the sixteenth and seventeenth centuries civic authorities increasingly addressed themselves to the problem of poverty and took steps to reorganize their systems of poor relief, perhaps also initiating schemes to provide employment. To do so they needed to know the scale of the problem. The Salisbury census of the poor of 1625 was associated with the introduction, by a group of puritan councillors, of a 'New Scheme' for the poor and a further survey was taken in the town roughly ten years later.[7] The information which was noted in such surveys was the number of people in a household, their ages, occupations – including those of children who worked – their weekly income and the poor relief which they were receiving. A census of the poor in Ipswich taken in 1597 also noted their needs: money, bedding, clothing, candles or perhaps working materials and implements.[8] Such records provide information on household size and structure, the proportion of wives who undertook paid work, the ages at which children were employed, the trades in which paupers were engaged – which might reflect an industry in decline or simply one that produced low remuneration – and the circumstances and numbers of those who were actually receiving relief. The Ipswich census lacks three parishes, but in towns for which there is a complete coverage the geographical distribution of the poor can be plotted. The Norwich census of the poor taken in 1570 is the most comprehensive record of this kind for the early modern period. It notes 2,342 men, women and children in the city and, in addition to the kind of information outlined above, indicates those children who were at school and the places from which immigrants had come to Norwich. To take just one example, Thomas Pele and his wife had arrived from Yorkshire nine years before the census was taken. He was a cobbler who was in work, she a spinner of white warp – a common occupation of the poor women in the city – and their eldest son, who was 16, was also engaged in spinning, while their other two sons, of 12 and 6, went to school. The age of both parents was given as 50. They did not receive relief, but were 'verie pore'.[9] Only a few such enumerations survive, but statements regarding the numbers of poor are fairly common in administrative records and petitions, and some of them are precise. It may be that the figures given in such statements were derived from similar kinds of enumerations.

## Ecclesiastical returns

A number of early-modern sources which contain demographic evidence had an ecclesiastical origin. The earliest of them are the chantry certificates, which were returned as part of the arrangements for the dissolution of the chantries, a process that was initiated by an Act of Parliament of 1545 and continued by another Act in 1547. They were completed by the parish clergy and churchwardens and include a figure for 'housling people', that is, the communicants. Age of first communion was then roughly 14 years. Precise numbers may have been difficult to achieve in populous urban parishes and, while some clergymen and their churchwardens perhaps attempted some kind of enumeration, others could have contented themselves with an estimate based upon their knowledge of their congregations and of the parish. There is certainly some doubt about the completeness and accuracy of the returns. The figures for the Oxfordshire market towns are inconsistent, with quite different numbers in the two series of certificates returned before and after Easter 1548. Only for Woodstock were the figures at all similar; at Burford the return rose from 544 to 1,000 and at Witney it increased from 800 to 1,100, while at Henley there was a decrease from 1,000 to 500 communicants.[10] This may indicate differing interpretations of what was required, or a greater awareness of the purpose of the returns, but in any case the roundness of the figures suggests that a broad approximation was regarded as fulfilling the requirement. The certificates are in class E 301 in the Public Record Office, Chancery Lane.

Returns survive for three large-scale ecclesiastical enumerations of the sixteenth and seventeenth centuries. The first was produced by a directive from the Privy Council to the bishops in 1563 to supply the numbers of families. The others date from 1603 and 1676, and both required the clergy to provide the numbers of anglican communicants, protestant nonconformists and catholic recusants in their parishes. It may be that individual clergymen were anxious to minimize the numbers of their parishioners who did not take the Anglican communion. Moreover, it is clear from the 1676 returns – the so-called Compton Census – that the requirement was interpreted in different ways, with the numbers of men or of families, even the total population, returned from some parishes. These problems are considered by Anne Whiteman in *The Compton*

*Census of 1676: A Critical Edition* (1986), which contains the figures for 1676, with the comparable ones from 1603 and the Protestation Returns of 1641–2. This edition also has tabulated estimates for the market towns for 1603 and 1676 alongside the figures from the 1811 census. The Compton Census covers only the province of Canterbury, while the returns for 1603 survive for four dioceses, and those for 1563 for eight dioceses in full and two others in part. The British Library's Harleian MSS 594, 595 and 618 contain the majority of the 1563 and 1603 returns, the Gloucester diocese material from 1563 is in the Bodleian at Rawlinson MS c.790 and that for 1603 relating to Lincoln is in the Lincolnshire record office. Survival of the Protestation Returns has also been patchy. Those which do exist are in the House of Lords record office and are listed in the appendix to the Historical Manuscripts Commission's *Fifth Report*. They contain the names of men over 18 taking the oath appended to the Protestation, a document devised in Parliament during the political crisis preceding the Civil War, which included an undertaking to uphold the reformed protestant religion. Those who did not take the oath were also named, but it may be doubted whether all men came forward or were approached, especially in the more populous urban parishes. For one Worcester parish, those who were away and 'cannot conveniently be at home by the tyme that we must returne these same' constituted 8.5 per cent of the names listed, and such absentees may be completely missing from other returns.[11] Nor can there be any certainty that the specified age threshold was strictly adhered to. Similarly, the age at which communion was first taken was neither rigid nor unchanging, apparently rising somewhat during the early modern period, causing some difficulty both in comparing the ecclesiastical enumerations from different dates and in converting the proportion of the population returned into estimates of its total size.

Parochial Easter Books record payment of the parishioners' obligatory annual contributions towards the maintenance of their incumbent. There was a considerable variety in the way in which the sum was assessed; in some parishes it was a poll tax on householders or communicants, in others it was related to rents, and in some cases it was based upon an assessment of tradesmen's profits. The basic information that can be gleaned from the Books is the number of households, but due allowance has to be made for those householders who were receiving parish alms and so presumably were exempt from payment. Wives and other communicants in the household may be noted, perhaps with some indication of their relationship to its head, or their status, such as apprentice, servant or journeyman. Where enough information is provided, the Books do allow some analysis of household composition to be made, as well as estimates of population size and perhaps of social structure. The changes between collections can also be revealing. The Books for Christ Church, Bristol, for the mid 1570s are arranged topographically, with the householders listed by street, and indicate the impact of the outbreak of plague there in 1575, through both the mortality suffered and the temporary absence of those prosperous parishioners who left to escape the epidemic.[12] The fall in population because of the fire in Oxford in 1644 is illustrated by the Books for St Ebbs parish for 1644 and 1645, with 625 names recorded in the earlier Book and only 287 in the later one.[13] Such Books survive from the mid sixteenth to the mid eighteenth centuries amongst parish records, although a long unbroken series is rare. As they were generally compiled by the incumbent himself or by the churchwardens, who should have had a fairly intimate knowledge of a parish, they are probably a reasonably reliable source. The parish officers presumably provided the figures that are included in the returns made at episcopal visitations, but these are less informative and commonly give only the total numbers of families.

## Taxation returns

The major problems encountered when using taxation returns as social and demographic evidence are under-assessment and evasion. Because of the nature of taxation, early-modern tax records can only be expected to yield the relativities, not the absolutes, of personal wealth. Nor can it be assumed that the degree of under-assessment was constant, even at a particular collection, for the collectors in one town or district may have been more zealous and determined than those in another, and so comparisons between communities have to be interpreted cautiously. Evasion is an equally serious defect of such data, for, although valid exemptions may be listed in a tax return, there was a section of urban society which was able to escape official attention and so passed unrecorded. A further difficulty is that some tax returns were brought up-to-date only infrequently and, even then, previous lists may have been used as the basis of a 'new' listing. Only in the case of a new tax or a complete reassessment of an existing one can we be reasonably confident that such stagnation was avoided.

The lay subsidy returns of 1524 and 1525 were the outcome of a new survey which produced the most comprehensive tax record since the 1377–81 Poll Taxes. For that reason they have been used as a bench mark by historians of both the late medieval and early modern periods. The assessment was made upon the basis of an individual's chief form of wealth, whether personal property valued at at least £1, or an annual income of £1 or more from land or in wages. The names listed are those of male taxpayers over 16 years old and women who were heads of households. Those who did not qualify to pay the subsidy were not returned. A comparison of the 1522 muster lists with the subsidy records for Exeter and Leicester indicates that such non-payers constituted roughly one-third of the adult male population in those towns.[14] The proportion varied from place to place, however, for the subsidy was broadly related to prosperity and, in this respect, it is unfortunate that it was taken at a time of economic recession in many towns. A similar subsidy was levied in 1543, 1544 and 1545, although wage earners were then excluded, which may represent a significant omission in some towns. In addition to the taxpayers' names – which should not be equated with households – and the basis and sums on which they were assessed, a few returns also note the occupations of the taxpayers; this information is given for over 80 per cent of the names listed at Northampton in 1524. The data give some indication of the distribution of taxable wealth within a town – in some of the small clothing towns the bulk of the wealth was in very few hands – and provide comparisons between towns in terms of the numbers of taxpayers and assessed wealth. One difficulty with the national rankings based upon the 1524 and 1525 returns is that Wales, the four northern English counties, Cheshire and the Cinque Ports were exempt. Comparison of the 1520s assessments and those from the 1540s has to take account of the absence of wage earners from the latter. The subsequent subsidies are less valuable, for they were levied from smaller sections of the population and the relationship between actual and assessed wealth became very remote indeed.

The Poll Tax returns are a valuable record of this kind for the later Middle Ages; the collections of 1377, 1379 and 1381 generated the most complete taxation records of the period and incidentally helped to spark off a major rebellion. The tax was briefly revived under Henry VIII and again in 1641, it was levied three times during Charles II's reign – in 1660, 1667 and 1678 – and on four occasions between 1689 and its abolition in 1698. In the seventeenth century, all those aged 16 or over who were not receiving poor relief were liable to pay the tax, which was graduated according to wealth and social status. This is to state an elaborate structure in simple terms, however, and the returns reflect the complexity of the tax. Some of them contain children, for some, but not all, children were taxed. It is very difficult to allow for the various categories of exemptions, but the returns can be used as a guide to the presence of apprentices and servants in households, and the grading by wealth and status does provide evidence for the structure of an urban community and the relationship between wealth and occupations. A sample from the returns from the City of London for 1692 shows that 811 taxpayers were engaged in 143 specified occupations and that 431 of them were assessed to pay the surtax. Unsurprisingly, all of the vintners paid the surtax and the porters, always amongst the less well-off sections of society, all paid the basic 1s. 0d. rate.[15] It may be possible to deduce from the returns the use to which a particular building was being put. For instance, it seems likely that the one in the cathedral close at Worcester which contained 20 maidens in 1678 was being used as a girls' school.[16] One problem with using the returns is that not all of their compilers clearly related servants, apprentices and other residents who did not carry the householder's surname to the household in which they lived, making it difficult to establish the number and composition of separate households. The usefulness of the record is considerably diminished in such cases.

Two direct taxes introduced under the later Stuarts also generated potentially useful records. The Hearth Tax was derived from continental models and was particularly unpopular, partly because the collectors had the right to enter premises in order to ascertain the numbers of hearths. It was imposed in 1662 and abolished in 1689. Virtually all of the surviving records are from the years when the tax was collected by the King's Receivers, that is, from its inception until 1665 and from 1670 until 1674. During the intervening years and again until 1684 it was collected by tax farmers, and after 1684 by a joint Commission for the Excise and Hearth Money. Poor householders, almshouses and hospitals, and certain categories of industrial hearths were exempt from payment. It seems unlikely that separate houses could have escaped detection, but it is possible that in subdivided buildings in closely built-up neighbourhoods some households were overlooked, and the erratic numbers of hearths returned at different collections suggests that 'hearths' could be success-fully concealed, or that some collectors chose not to press their enquiries too closely. As with other taxes of the period, the extent of evasion is uncertain. The proportion of the households officially returned as exempt may be used as a rough index of the relative prosperity of urban communities. Such figures do show considerable differences between towns, from 18 per cent exempt at Cambridge, to 41 per cent at Newcastle-upon-Tyne, 53 per cent at Walsall and almost 62 per cent at Norwich, but conceal the local variations within each town.[17] For instance, 39 per cent of the recorded households in Warwick in 1670 were exempt, an average that was exceeded in only two of the eight wards. The proportions in the two poorest wards were 66 and 61 per cent and together they contained 137 of the 238 households in the town which were exempt.[18] Figures for the mean numbers of hearths per household can be used in a similar way, for they provide a general indication of relative prosperity and household size. Some of the more prominent buildings, such as inns, can be identified in the Hearth Tax returns, but only rarely can their topographical arrangement be traced. This also applies to surviving records for the Window Tax, which was introduced in 1696 and was continued, with modifications, by a number of statutes, the last of which was in 1808. It was abolished in 1851. The returns list the names of the householders, or others liable to pay, and the numbers of windows or the sums levied. Its local administration was generally unsatisfactory and there are, in any case, relatively few surviving lists. Those which are extant are to be found amongst local records, sometimes in association with returns for the duty on inhabited houses, which was introduced in 1778. The returns for the lay subsidies, Poll and Hearth taxes are in class E 179 at the Public Record Office, Chancery Lane, although many Poll Tax lists survive only in local collections. The whereabouts of these and other taxation lists of the period are given in J.S.W. Gibson, *The Hearth Tax, other late Stuart Tax Lists and the Association Oath Rolls* (1985).

The records generated by the Marriage Duties Act of 1694 are potentially the most valuable of all the early-modern taxation returns, from a demographic viewpoint. The Act imposed a basic levy on all births and burials and also a complex scale of payments, based upon social and economic status, for marriages. Bachelors over 25 years old and childless widowers were also taxed and although those receiving poor relief were exempt from the fees payable for births and marriages, payment had to be made for their burials. The implementation of the tax required a listing of the population as well as a comprehensive record of births, marriages and burials, and to that end Quakers, Roman Catholics and Jews were directed to provide notification of those events. This should have produced an annual enumeration of the population in all parishes for the years 1695–1706, during which the tax was levied, with a record of the composition of households and the structure of at least a part of society, for the status or trade of many householders was noted. Unfortunately, none of the Exchequer's returns now exists and survival of the parochial copies has been sporadic. Amongst those which are extant are those for Bristol, 1696, for 117 London parishes for 1695 and for five parishes in Southampton for 1695–7. In addition to the surviving documents, there are Gregory King's data which were derived from the returns, such as those for Lichfield, Tiverton, Gloucester and Norwich.[19] The tax was not well received. In John Evelyn's parish the parishioners' names were read out after divine service: in his views it was 'a very imprudent & impertinent dutch Tax and especialy this reading the names, so most went out of all the Churches'.[20] In the small and well administered parishes the returns may have been fairly accurate, despite such hostility, but in some of the more populous ones, with a relatively rapid turnover of population, they were probably incomplete. Nevertheless, the surviving material generated by this taxation-cum-enumeration provides valuable demographic evidence: it is possible that Gregory King had a hand in devising the measure, with just that objective in mind.

King's evidence for the 1690s and other listings of inhabitants from the early modern period have been used to establish demographic characteristics which can be employed to convert figures derived from ecclesiastical enumerations and taxation records into estimates of population size. His data suggest a mean household size in 'cities and market towns' of 4.4 persons. This is rather lower than the standard of 4.75 persons which appears to have been the norm for all communities in early modern England, but is closer to the mean household size of 4.25 persons that is applicable during the period of stagnating national population in the late seventeenth and early eighteenth centuries.[21] This phase of stagnation, indeed of slight decline, followed one of sustained population growth that lasted from the early sixteenth century until the 1650s. A concomitant of demographic stagnation was a relatively small proportion of children and adolescents in the population; perhaps one-third of urban inhabitants in the late seventeenth century were under 16 years old.[22] On this basis a multiplier of 1.5 should be applied to the figures for adults contained in the Compton Census and one of 3.0, or slightly higher, to those for adult men in the Protestation Returns. Such multipliers are necessarily generalizations derived from aggregate data, and an accurate assessment of population size has to be related to a town's circumstances when the enumeration or tax return was compiled. One with a prospering economy and an expanding population was likely to contain both a relatively high percentage of young people and a larger than average household size, while one which was stagnating or in decline would probably have a population displaying the opposite characteristics. The study of urban population cannot be undertaken without reference to economic and social conditions within the community being examined.

## Parish registers and bills of mortality

In 1538 Thomas Cromwell, as Vicar General, ordered that a record be kept of the baptisms, marriages and burials in every parish. Sixty years later a royal injunction instructed that such records should be kept on parchment; it further directed that incumbents were to transcribe all earlier ones into the new parchment volumes and henceforth return annual copies to the diocesan registry – the so-called bishops' transcripts. Survival of both original parish registers and transcripts has been very irregular and few parishes have records that actually begin in the mid-sixteenth century. Access to surviving registers has been facilitated by the order of 1978 that all those over 100 years old and not in use should be deposited at the appropriate diocesan record office.

Although the information required by Cromwell's order was simple enough, there was considerable variation in the way in which it was recorded, some clerks or incumbents noting baptisms, marriages and burials separately and others entering them in a continuous chronological sequence. In some registers the dates of birth and death were noted, as well as the required ones of baptism and burial. Uniformity came only with Rose's Act of Parliament of 1812, which ordered that parish registers were to be kept in books of standard forms provided by the King's printers. Civil registration of births, deaths and marriages was introduced 25 years later and the resultant records are kept at St Catherine's House in London. Added to these problems of inconsistency are doubts about the accuracy and completeness of parochial record keeping. Small urban parishes providing low stipends were frequently held in plurality and neglected by their incumbents. The entries in the registers may not have been made up regularly so errors and omissions may have occurred, especially during epidemics. At Holywell in Oxford during the 1660s and 1670s the register was kept by a 'drunken carless clerke' who was 'a notoriouse sot'.[23] Other omissions arose from the fact that it was the readings of the appropriate services which were recorded, not the actual events of birth and death. Unbaptized infants were not entitled to have the burial service read over them and so would pass completely unrecorded; although age at baptism was normally only a few days before the end of the seventeenth century, it was more variable thereafter and the proportion of births which was omitted was perhaps correspondingly larger.[24] Suicides also passed without mention in the register, for they, too, were not entitled to be buried according to the rites of the established church. Nevertheless, the burials of suicides and unbaptized infants may have been silently included in the registers. A more serious deficiency is the absence of Roman Catholics and protestant dissenters from the registers, especially in those towns where nonconformity was strong. Although both catholics and dissenters increasingly kept their own registers, there is commonly something of a hiatus before they begin. Most surviving dissenters' registers are now kept at the Public Record Office. It seems that the 40 years or so after 1780 were a period during which anglican registration was especially defective, because urban population growth was outstripping new church building, producing densely populated parishes, and there was also a major revival of nonconformity during those years.[25]

Monthly and annual totals of vital events can be used to illustrate demographic change. The data for marriages tend to be rather erratic, but those for baptisms and burials – or births and deaths if distinguished – indicate the patterns of fertility and mortality and also suggest changes in the size of the population. They are not a satisfactory source from which to obtain a figure for its total size. Burials exceeded baptisms in many urban parishes during the pre-modern period and the population was maintained by inward migration. This was particularly true during times of epidemic, which are readily identifiable from the high numbers of burials and probably also from some indication in the registers of the cause of death, with plague and smallpox victims being distinguished, for example. The seasonality of mortality is also suggestive of the nature of an epidemic, plague being most virulent during the summer months. When a husband or wife was a victim of an epidemic, the surviving partner often remarried and perhaps began a new family, and so successive peaks of burials, marriages and baptisms occur in the registers. As well as providing information from the aggregate data, parish registers can also be used, in conjunction with wills, for family reconstitution and examination of connections between families in the business and political spheres within the community.

A characteristic of the registers of many urban parishes is that, to further identify individuals in populous parishes, their status or trade was entered when their children were baptized and buried and when they themselves were buried, before this became a standard entry in registers in 1812. As all members of the Church of England ought to have appeared in the registers at some stage in their lives, unless their stay in a parish was short, the registers should provide a good occupational profile of the population, and a dynamic one from which changes can be traced, rather than a picture at a particular date of the kind provided by census and tax returns. A potential problem is that young immigrants to a town may have served an apprenticeship and, after a few years of independent operation, have left to practise their trade elsewhere; if they did not start a family during this formative stage of their adult lives they would not appear in the parish registers. Average age of first marriage for men in the seventeenth and eighteenth centuries was roughly 26 and of women two years less.[26] A further drawback in using registers for this purpose is that a particular trade may have been dominated by a section of the community outside the Church of England and so not be represented in the occupational profile. Other sources, such as title deeds, may indicate whether this was the case.

More detailed information on the causes of death is available from bills of mortality for London and the larger provincial cities. These were devised in the early sixteenth century with the object of tracing the incidence of plague and so giving some indications of the beginnings of an epidemic. Survival from before 1600 is generally patchy and indeed the bills were initially kept only intermittently, but on the other hand they outlasted their original purpose and continued to be compiled after plague had been eradicated. Some remained in manuscript form, others were issued as printed broadsheets, and the early London newspapers carried statistics for the capital and some other towns. The weekly London series continued nominally to 1837, although some were prepared as late as 1852. The parishes covered by the London bills came to be regarded as the metropolitan area, for statistical purposes. The bills were compiled from information returned by the parish clerks and, as with the bishops' transcripts, errors occurred in the process and the bills are not an entirely accurate summary of the original registers. Totals of baptisms in the London bills for the eighteenth century under-record the registers' figures by roughly 7 per cent, for example.[27] Deaths are subdivided by age groups and the causes categorized, allowing a much closer analysis of mortality patterns than is possible from the registers alone.

## Probate inventories and wills

Probate inventories were drawn up between the mid sixteenth and late eighteenth centuries for the purpose of administering the estate of a deceased person, being designed to protect the executors or administrators from excessive claims upon the estate and to safeguard the beneficiaries against fraud. They were also used as the basis for the calculation of the probate court's fees. The inventories were proved with wills and administration bonds in the ecclesiastical courts and are to be found in the diocesan record offices. Estates valued at less than 50s. 0d. were not inventoried and so a considerable section of the urban population is not represented in the inventory record; at the other end of the economic scale, the inventories of those exceeding £1,500, or which were held in more than one diocese, were proved in the Prerogative Court of Canterbury. The occupation or status of the deceased is commonly given in the heading of the document, together with his or her parish of residence. It may be possible to identify a more precise address from information given in the inventory itself, the deceased's will or other sources.

An inventory consists of a list of the personal estate of the deceased – real estate was not included – and contains such items as apparel, furniture, domestic utensils, trade goods and debts. Household goods were usually listed by room and in many documents were individually itemized and valued (pp. 44–6). The inventories can be used to examine the wealth of townsmen, comparing the estates of the various groups within the urban population, such as retailers, manufacturers and those engaged in victualling. The proportion of wealth held in household goods, stock in trade and tools and equipment is a good indication of the deceased's economic interests. Inventory valuations also illustrate changes in material comforts and prosperity through time, due allowance being made for the effects of inflation. The appraisers of some inventories lumped all the debts owing to the deceased together in a single entry, but others itemized each debt and perhaps noted the place and trade of the debtor, thereby giving an insight into the extent and nature of the deceased's economic connections.

Inventories survive for those who made wills and those who died intestate, although in fewer numbers than wills and administration bonds. Where a will and an inventory survive for the same estate they should be used in conjunction and, fortunately, it was the practice of most probate courts to file the two documents together. The testator may have mentioned some of his or her property in directing how it should be disposed, but in many cases the bulk of an estate was left to one person, the spouse, a son or daughter, and so it was not described. Those items which were individually bequeathed were, most commonly, only a few of the most valued personal and household items. As in inventories, wills may contain a mention or even a list of debts owed to the deceased. Although wills contain only an incomplete record of the contents of estates, the practice of leaving some items, even small tokens, to members of the family makes them invaluable for family reconstitution and the identification of urban dynasties.

Inventories and wills can be used to examine the occupational structure of a town, but with the important proviso that only a part of the population is represented in the probate records. It may be difficult to establish the size and typicality of that part of the community which produced records of this kind. A wider social range should have been represented in the inventories as the inflation of the sixteenth and early seventeenth centuries gradually increased the proportion of the population which owned personal estates worth more than the threshold figure. Yet the relatively small numbers of inventories which do survive can only record a few of those town dwellers with such estates. Probate documents are deposited in the appropriate diocesan repository, which is a county record office in many cases, and those of the Prerogative Court of Canterbury are in the Public Record Office in Chancery Lane. They can be located from J.S.W. Gibson, *Wills and Where to Find Them* (1974) and A.J. Camp, *Wills and their Whereabouts* (1974)

## Apprentice and freemen registers

Freemen of a city or borough were entitled to trade within the corporation free of tolls, to sit on the council and perhaps to vote in corporation and parliamentary elections. Admission to the freedom could be obtained in four ways. The first was by serving an apprenticeship with a freeman for a term which should have been at least seven years. The apprentices were registered with the corporation, which kept a record giving the apprentice's name and age, his father's name and place of residence, the master to whom the apprentice was bound, with his trade, and the length of the term. Subsequent transfers to other masters were also enrolled. The corporation's record may be incomplete, for the apprentices in the poorer trades may not have registered, thereby saving the fee which was levied. Such apprentices presumably wished to learn the trade in order to practise it elsewhere and they did not aspire to the freedom. Enforcement of registration was liable to fluctuate, partly because it was a source of revenue for the corporation, whose financial needs varied. The craft or guild companies maintained similar registers of those who were apprenticed to their members. The indentures or contracts between the master and the apprentices' parents or guardians give fuller information on the actual terms of the arrangement and the fee involved, and these may have survived, especially if they were produced as evidence in the event of a dispute during the term of the apprenticeship. Such disputes were heard in the civic courts or by the officers of the guild, and the minutes of such hearings may contain much incidental information on the actual operation of the system. Secondly, freedom could be obtained by patrimony, for the sons of freemen were entitled to claim citizenship. In some boroughs this privilege extended to someone who married a freeman's daughter or widow. Thirdly, the right could be purchased, with the consent of the corporation. Fourthly, freedom could be granted by the corporation, as an honorary award to a distinguished person or patron, or in recognition of useful services rendered. Such grants were recorded in the common council's minutes.

Registers of all freemen admitted distinguish the mode of entry to the freedom. Comparison with the apprenticeship registers shows the extent of the wastage of those who were entered as apprentices but failed to achieve the freedom. Exeter corporation kept a record of those apprentices who were 'rejected as freemen for misbehaviour and other causes'.[28] The places of origin of apprentices and freemen created by grant can be used to trace the area from which a town was drawing its labour, and the information on parental status can indicate the background from which apprentices to a particular trade came. The trades mentioned in the registers give some indication of occupational structure, but this evidence can be misleading, for a freeman may have changed his occupation due to economic or personal circumstances after his admission and, because of terminological inexactitude, the registers may only give the categories of employment, rather than the trades which were actually being practised. Apprenticeship provided the means of entry to the freedom, it did not bind a man to follow a trade for life. The system declined from the late seventeenth century and gradually fell into abeyance as an effective way of controlling the operation of labour within a corporation. Nevertheless, registers of apprentices and freemen continued to be kept and admissions to the freedom were still sought and granted, partly because of the revenue which corporations derived from the fees and partly because of the voting rights which were associated with freemen status.

## Poll-books

A list of those who held the right to vote was compiled for some elections before the end of the seventeenth century and should have been kept for all contested parliamentary elections after the Act of Parliament of 1696, which was designed to regulate the conduct of such polls. The resultant poll-books are an important source until they cease with the coming of the secret ballot in 1872. They have survived in a number of forms: as separate documents, in a volume kept for that or for a miscellany of purposes, within a variety of publications, including newspapers, or as separate printed booklets. Lists of voters were compiled not only for parliamentary contests, but for municipal and parochial elections as well. The arrangement of the contents varies, but typically a poll-book consists of a list of all those who were eligible to vote, distinguishing those who lived outside the borough, and indicating how they cast their votes, with the result of the poll. The names of the resident voters may be arranged alphabetically, but more commonly they are listed by ward or parish, or even by street, and their occupations are also given. The value of poll-books as a guide to occupational structure is, however, limited by the fact that only one section of the population is represented in them, that is, those adult males who could vote. Their numbers were controlled by the nature of the franchise. In some towns it was the householders who were entitled to vote and so the poll-books cover a wide range of the adult male population. This was the case at Northampton and in 1768 many non-householders there also managed to vote, albeit illegally, and hence the poll-book for that election contains a large proportion of the town's adult males.[29] The franchises in other towns were restricted to the freemen or to those occupying certain plots of ground which carried the right to vote. It was not uncommon for there to be a number of freemen created just before an election, a practice which can be traced in the freemen's registers and perhaps in the councils' minutes. Such recent creations may even be listed separately in the poll-book itself. Generally, poll-books under-record such groups as labourers and servants. In addition to the information which poll-books provide for occupational structure, they are also invaluable for the political evidence which they contain, indicating the nature of loyalties and groupings within a town and, from a series of books, their durability or fragility.

## Militia returns

The militia returns were generated in response to the requirements of the Militia Act of 1757, which was subsequently modified by a number of amending Acts. The returns should be amongst the official papers of the Lords Lieutenant, or in the corporation archives. The parish officers, usually the constables, were required to make a return of those men who were of age to serve in the militia. The specified age range was from 18 to 45, although in the amending Act of 1803 this was extended to the 17 to 55 age group. Amongst those who were exempt from service were those who were infirm or had some physical disability, clergymen, licensed teachers, medical practitioners, articled clerks, apprentices, seamen and the parish constables themselves. There was also an exemption for poor men with children; in 1757 this was fixed at three or more legitimate children, but it was reduced to one child in 1786. The returns typically list the names, ages and occupations of the men within the specified age range and perhaps note any disabilities, those who were already serving in the volunteers and an indication of willingness to serve. Some returns contain more than this basic information, giving actual ages and perhaps including parishioners outside the group liable for service. That for the parish of St Mary Steps, Exeter, for 1803 enumerates all the men, women and children up to the age of 60, and also the livestock in the parish, which apparently consisted of 9 horses, 58 pigs and 24 bullocks.[30]

The value of the returns as a record of occupational structure is dependant on their completeness. The constables may not have been particularly diligent in discovering occupations that were not already known to them, resulting in gaps in the record. For example, 15 per cent of the men named in the returns for Exeter for 1803 are not assigned an occupation or status. More importantly, the returns may not include some or all of those who were entitled to exemption, because the constables silently omitted them. The returns are likely to under-record gentry and members of the professions. The upper age limit could also produce an inaccurate picture of employment patterns by under-recording trades which, although still practised, were in decline and were being carried on largely by men who were too old for militia service. On the other hand, labourers and servants, who are not well represented in poll-books, should appear in the militia lists. Militia returns cannot provide a complete picture of the occupational profile of the adult male population of towns, but they do supply valuable evidence for the late eighteenth and early nineteenth centuries, before other, more comprehensive, sources become available.

# Chapter Five
# POPULATION AND SOCIETY FROM 1800

Although there is no abrupt change in the types of sources from which urban demography and society can be studied, some of those that are available for the nineteenth and twentieth centuries are of a rather different nature from those which have to be drawn upon for the earlier periods. This is partly because the wish to obtain accurate statistics on the size and composition of the population and the growing concern with public health and sanitation produced material of a kind and on a scale which is not available for towns from before the end of the eighteenth century. The national decennial censuses, instituted in 1801, and the various social and sanitary investigations reflect these concerns. Other sources, such as parish registers, bills of mortality, wills and poll-books, retain their value, but few probate inventories were compiled after the end of the eighteenth century and freemen and apprenticeship registers ceased to have any validity at around that time.

One potential difficulty with an attempt to trace population changes in a town over a long period is that the units used for enumeration may have differed from one source to another and their boundaries were changed from time to time. This applied both to the units within the administrative area of a town and to the boundaries of that area. The inclusion of districts previously outside a town can give the impression of a rapid rise of population, which was a reflection of administrative, not demographic, change. This difficulty is most acute for periods of rapid urbanization, when boundary changes commonly lagged well behind the growth of a town which was spreading outwards into the surrounding parishes. The converse problem arises for many towns in the north of England which grew rapidly after the onset of industrialization, for they were set within very large parishes, each of which contained a number of separate communities. Changes in the boundaries of the enumeration districts employed in the national census returns are recorded, but making correct allowances for such changes may, in practice, prove to be rather difficult.

## Commercial directories

The origins of directories can be traced to a list of London merchants that was issued in 1677, although it was another 55 years before a further

69

directory of that kind was produced. Separate directories for provincial cities first appeared in the 1760s and 1770s and they were evidently a success, for they had been published for the majority of the cities and larger towns by the early nineteenth century. The smaller towns which did not warrant a separate directory were included in the county or regional ones. Directories were frequently reissued, but not always after careful corrections and updating had been carried out, so that errors were perpetuated and the names of residents could still be listed some time after they had moved or died.

Directories were designed primarily for use by the business and commercial community. This was reflected in the kind of information which they carried on, for example, the banks which were represented in a town, its coaching and, later, railway services. It became a common practice to include a plan of the town. The major part of a directory was the list of businesses and residents, with their occupations and statuses. Personal names were arranged in alphabetical or some form of topographical order, or with the practitioners of a particular trade, craft or service grouped together. Addresses were also supplied and so the distribution of each speciality within a town can be traced. Seven of the 12 ropemakers listed in Liverpool in Gore's 1766 directory were clustered close to each other along the Manchester road, for example.[1] From such evidence the various elements can be plotted on a town plan, which should show the location of the commercial, legal and industrial quarters and the principal shopping streets. The lists of residents were selective, however, and only a minority of the inhabitants were included. The basis of the selection was related chiefly to the directories' function of supplying information that was useful for those in business, but by no means all businesses were included in them; those in the main streets and thoroughfares were more likely to get an entry than those which were not. There was also something of a social criterion for inclusion; Raffald's directory for Manchester of 1772 claimed to include 'every Inhabitant of the least Consequence'.[2] Directories do not, therefore, provide an accurate picture of a town's overall occupational or social structure, but they do indicate its specialities and the diversity of trades, crafts and professions practised. This is especially useful evidence for the late eighteenth and early nineteenth centuries, before the 1841 census recorded such information. C.W.F. Goss, *The London Directories, 1677–1855* (1932) and J.E. Norton, *Guide to the National and Provincial Directories of England and Wales, excluding London, published before 1856* (1950, 1984) provide guides to the available directories up to the middle of the nineteenth century. The later period is covered by Gareth Shaw and Allison Tipper, *British Directories: A Bibliography and Guide to Directories Published in England and Wales (1850–1950) and Scotland (1773–1950)* (1989).

## Bankrupts, businesses and factories

Those who were unfortunate or less than fully capable in business were likely to reach the point where they became bankrupt. The Act 'for the relief of insolvent debtors' of 1712 required such debtors to place notices to their creditors in the *London Gazette* which, from that date, provides a list of those who were declared bankrupt.[3] The *Gentleman's Magazine*, which began publication in 1731, and newspapers, also carry notices of bankrupts. As well as identifying those individuals who became bankrupt, lists of bankrupts may suggest cycles of business prosperity in a town and groupings by occupation can indicate the periods of economic difficulty in particular trades and industries. The records of the Court of Bankruptcy and the proceedings under the earlier bankruptcy laws are in the Public Record Office, Chancery Lane. They begin in 1710 and include minutes and order books, and files of proceedings, with evidence presented in examinations and depositions. The Court of Judicature's records include, in class J 13, actions under the Companies (Winding-up) Proceedings from 1891 to 1948, with 19,052 files arranged by alphabetical order of company. Generally, business records go to local record offices or are retained by the companies or their successors. There is a guide to the whereabouts and contents of such records, mostly of those companies registered in the 1870s and 1880s, their subsidiaries and associated businesses, in Lesley Richmond and Bridget Stockford, *Company Archives: The Survey of the Records of 1000 of the First Registered Companies in England and Wales* (1986).

The administration created for implementing and enforcing the terms of the 1833 Factory Act initiated a body of evidence relating to the operation of industry and the social conditions of its workers. The principle of state intervention in regulating the conditions of factory operatives was established by the Health and Morals of Apprentices Act of 1802, but the early legislation, including the 1833 Act, was concerned chiefly with the employment of children and young people in factories. Only with the 1844 Factory Act and its successors was the scope of the legislation significantly widened and the problems of safety addressed. By the terms of the Act of 1833, children aged 9 to 13 were to work no more than 9 hours per day and a 12–hour day was specified for those between 13 and 18. The Act also introduced compulsory education for the 9 to 13 year olds who were working in factories. It applied to cotton, woollen and worsted, hemp, flax, tow and linen mills, but not to lace factories, and it had only limited application in silk mills. Most significantly, the 1833 Act created a full-time inspectorate to monitor the implementation of its terms.[4] The *Minutes* of the inspectors' meetings and their *Reports* to the Home Office, presented as Parliamentary Papers, detail their operations and findings. This material contains notices of breaches of the legislation on child labour, health and safety, and of accidents, new factory growth, the introduction of machinery and industrial developments, with tables of the factories visited and the numbers of their employees – from which the scale of employment can be deduced – and more detailed information on specific factories. The early *Reports* contain depositions which illustrate working practices and the development of the factory system.[5]

The Factory Inspectors and their superintendants found it especially difficult to enforce the educational provisions of the 1833 Act and much of their attention was concentrated on that problem. In addition to the summaries and recommendations in their regular *Reports*, the inspectors also produced, in 1839, *Reports on the Educational Provisions of the Factories Act* describing the general state of the factory schools and detailing particular examples. Educational provision was a concern of other official enquiries of the period investigating trades and employment. The *Reports from Assistant Handloom Weavers' Commissioners*, for example, contain a comprehensive account of education in Coventry in 1838, supplying the numbers and types of schools and the numbers of pupils attending them.[6] Such investigations provide statistical information on the populations of the towns reported on and evidence of their social and employment conditions.

## The General Register Office

The General Register Office was another important creation of the 1830s. It was established in 1837 to implement the civil registration of births, marriages and deaths, required by the Registration and Marriage Acts of the previous year. Under the system, which did not replace the parish registers, the local registrars and their superintendants were responsible for recording these vital events on standard forms, in volumes. Certified copies of the entries in their registers were returned to the Registrar General each quarter and he was thereby presented with a mass of demographic information, which he was required to produce as abstracts. This was done in *Annual Reports* and, from 1849, the *Quarterly Returns*. Because of the way in which the first two Registrars General interpreted their duties, these publications did more than simply present statistical summaries of the returns. These two men, Thomas Lister and George Graham, whose tenure of the post continued until 1879, presented both tabulations of the data and their comments on and interpretations of them, drawing attention to particular points which analysis of the figures had revealed. Nor did they confine themselves to the demographic characteristics which their material displayed: they also examined its implications regarding social and health matters, aware that they could influence government policy. Furthermore, they instituted enquiries of their own to supplement the evidence of the returns and assembled various economic indicators to set alongside their demographic ones. The *Annual Reports* and *Quarterly Returns* contain a range of evidence relating to the population and health of Victorian cities and towns, with particular aspects of individual places drawn upon as examples, such as the summary of the causes of deaths in road accidents in London, 1869–73, which was included in the *Annual Report* for 1873.[7] In addition, in 1840 the Office began to issue weekly returns of deaths in London, arranged by cause of death and age groups, to which births were added five years later, and similar returns were subsequently produced for the outer districts of the capital and for other large towns. It should be noted, however, that it was some years before the registration system introduced in 1837 achieved a complete record of all births and deaths. Indeed, problems of under-recording and the use of imprecise terms in noting the cause of death, were not entirely resolved until 1874.

## National censuses

The national censuses were inaugurated in 1801 and have been conducted at ten yearly intervals since then, with the sole exception of 1941. They have been carried out under the Registrar General's direction since 1841. The censuses got off to a shaky start, for the figures of 1801 were not especially reliable and were regarded as doubtful by the man who was in charge of the first four censuses, John Rickman. It is also possible that some erroneous returns were submitted at the later censuses, because of enumerators' errors, or evasion. The information required in 1801 was very basic, merely the numbers of people, divided by gender, the numbers of inhabited and uninhabited houses and the categorization of the workforce into very broad occupational groups. The subsequent censuses collected greater information on occupations, but even in 1831 the classification still only provided for seven divisions: agriculture, industrial labourers, manufacturing, professional, retailing, servants, and others. The first four censuses are, in any case, blunt instruments for urban historians, for they survive only in the form of statistical summaries, apart from a few enumerators' returns in local records.

The 1841 census is significant in two ways: it is the first one for which the actual schedules survive, and for the first time householders had to complete the census form. The returns for 1841 give the names of the people, the precise ages of children under 15 and for the remainder of the population rounded down to multiples of five, and each individual's occupation or status. Unfortunately, the requirement regarding occupation was not interpreted consistently and it is not certain that the information is provided for all adults in employment, rather than just heads of households or adult males. The 1841 census is also ambiguous in the separation of households where a house was occupied by more than one household. This problem is removed in the 1851 and later returns, which have a column in which each individual's relationship to the head of the household is entered. They also have precise figures for everyone's age and an entry for the place or country of birth.

The items of information recorded in the returns can be used to reconstruct the structure of Victorian households in terms of, for example, the ages of residents, the proportion of households headed by women, the numbers and ages of children and the proportion of households containing servants, lodgers or apprentices. The data on occupations and statuses can be used in a similar way, to identify the social characteristics of a street or neighbourhood, to discover if there was a dominant local trade, or immigrant group, to examine the relationship between gender and jobs, the age ranges of workers and the ages and proportion of children who attended school. There is, however, one drawback in using the censuses of 1841–1911 for an analysis of economic structure, which is that those employed as, for instance, engineers, factory workers, clerks, messengers or labourers, were classified in those terms and not assigned to the type of industry or other enterprise in which they worked. Used in conjunction with the contemporary large-scale Ordnance Survey plans, the returns provide the evidence for house repopulation, incidentally showing the distribution of family shops and businesses. Many entries on place of birth are imprecise, yet this is more reliable data than is available from any other source and may be exploited in order to trace patterns of rural–urban and inter-urban migration. The census returns are, however, closed to public access for 100 years. Those for 1841 and 1851 are in class HO 107, and for 1861, 1871 and 1881 in RG 9, 10, 11, amongst the public records and are also available on microfilm in many local libraries and record offices.

The Parliamentary Papers contain the reports and abstracts of tables which were issued after each of the censuses, their scale growing as the number of items of information collected increased. The population totals are tabulated in the general volumes of the *Victoria County Histories* and they provide an accessible source for tracing population changes, although caution is required in the interpretation of the figures because of changes in the units of enumeration. Tabulation of the aggregate figures from the returns and correlations of the various items collected appear in the abstracts. The 1891 census was the first one to record the numbers of rooms per house, which provided data for analysis of the number of rooms per household, occupancy rates per room and the proportion of small houses in a town. The statistics presented in the abstracts are arranged by census units, which may be rather unwieldy for local studies, and, by cutting across economic and social divisions, perhaps be rather misleading. The reports summarize the findings and draw some conclusions from the censuses. For example, the general report on the 1901 census identified the greatest growth points in the urban population over the previous decade, which had been in the suburban areas and medium-sized towns, rather than within the cities and larger towns.

## Education and religious censuses

In 1834 John Rickman, turning his attention to education, estimated that 1,276,947 children in England attended day schools and 271,943 more than that went to Sunday schools. He arrived at these figures on the basis of replies from the 15,000 circulars which he had sent out to overseers. His enquiry prompted local investigations by the statistical societies (p. 78), which demonstrated that his figures were serious underestimates. For example, in Manchester, Rickman's returns had missed 181 schools and between 8,000 and 9,000 scholars. A more complete enumeration was attempted in 1851, when an educational survey was undertaken with the national census. The returns were incomplete, the original forms are lost and only the figures in the census reports are available. These show that 2,144,378 children were at some kind of school, but they also leave approximately 1,000,000 unaccounted for, not recorded as being at school or at work.

The 1851 census was also accompanied by an investigation of places of worship and attendances at them. It had been preceded by an enquiry that had been set on foot by the House of Commons in 1829 to determine 'the number of Places of Worship, not of the Church of England, in each parish; distinguishing, as far as possible, of what sect or persuasion, and the total number of each sect in England and Wales'. Only the returns for Lancashire were printed, in the Parliamentary Papers for 1830, and the original returns were probably destroyed in the fire at the Houses of Parliament in 1834. Copies of the returns were kept by some of the Clerks of the Peace, who were responsible for submitting the originals, and they have survived, amongst their papers, for Essex, Hertfordshire, Lancashire, the parts of Kesteven in Lincolnshire, Nottinghamshire, Sussex and Wiltshire. They supply much incidental information, such as the numbers attending worship, but may not be completely reliable. Nevertheless, they are valuable for giving some indication of the strength of nonconformity in the towns and the relative support for the various denominations.[8]

The information required in 1851 was the date of the church or chapel building, the uses, other than for worship, to which it was put, the number of sittings, free and otherwise, the size of the congregations on 30 March and the average numbers attending. The date chosen was that of the census. The returns provide evidence of the variety and relative strength of the denominations in a town. The proportion of the population which attended services on the census day is less certain, for it was the number of attendances, not of attenders, that was recorded. It is not possible to determine the numbers who went to more than one service during the day. There was also a section for 'remarks', which reveals that in Lincoln the attendances at the evening service on 30 March were smaller than usual because a heavy thunderstorm, just as people were preparing to set out, deterred some would-be worshippers. Such events were likely to affect the numbers and give a misleading impression of the size of the congregations which the required average figures did not entirely correct, partly because the clergy were not used to keeping a record of the numbers attending and may have had only a vague idea of the size of an average congregation. A few misunderstood the requirement and returned other figures, the numbers of baptisms, for example; perhaps because that was the only hard data which they actually had. Not all of the enquiries were answered, some columns of the forms being left blank.

The section inviting 'remarks' elicited some information of a kind which provides useful insights into this aspect of mid-nineteenth-century urban life. The Wesleyan Methodist Reformers' chapel in Grantham had been converted from a theatre in the previous year. It had 700 sittings, 310 of them free, and standing space for a further 100. On the morning of 30 March there were 418 in the congregation, 120 children attended the Sunday school, both in the morning and afternoon, and 686 worshippers went to the evening service. The average attendance over the previous six months had been 600; this in a town with a population of 5,375. In addition to this numerical information was the statement, 'The reason why the chapel has been opened is, some of the leaders were "expelled" from the society at Finkin Street which the majority of the church members considered contrary to Old Wesleyan rules and contrary to Scripture if not contrary to the law of the land'. Indeed, the return for the Finkin Street chapel admitted that the congregation there was 'pretty diminished'.[9]

The returns were numbered in parish order, using the same system as the general census, and then entered into books, now held as class HO 129 at the Public Record Office at Kew. The official *Report* by Horace Mann was produced as a Parliamentary Paper in 1854. This investigation was not regarded as a success and was suspected of giving a misleading impression of affiliations. In particular, critics pointed out that the survey was undertaken on just one day, when the weather or other factors may have affected attendances, that it was conducted by the clergy themselves and that it was an estimate rather than a head count. The attendances recorded indicated that the numbers of churchgoers were small, very small in some of the industrial cities, and this was unwelcome information as far as the ecclesiastical authorities were concerned.

The enquiry was not repeated at later censuses, but individual diocesan investigations were carried out from time to time. The 1851 returns did serve as a stimulus for other, unofficial, enquiries, which sought to improve on its methods. They were conducted by a variety of individuals and groups in a number of towns in the late nineteenth and early twentieth centuries. A series that was carried out in 1881–2 was summarized by Andrew Mearns in *The Statistics of Attendance at Public Worship, 1881–2* (1882). The results of other private investigations of the same kind were generally reported in local newspapers. Two of the more ambitious such enquiries were undertaken in London. The earlier one, in 1886, was taken under the auspices of the *British Weekly* on 24 October. It provided the example for a larger-scale attempt organized by the *Daily News* in 1902–3, which was extended over a year, but excluding August, in an attempt to overcome the unrepresentativeness of returns made on a single Sunday. The results were published in R. Mudie-Smith, *The Religious Life of London* (1904), which includes the figures for 1886. It was undertaken by place of worship, distinguishing morning and evening services and also men, women and children under 15. By including all masses and communions throughout the day, it sought to provide a full total for the numbers of worshippers. It also contains a list of 2,688 places of worship, including 62 synagogues. Seebohm Rowntree's numbers of adult church attenders, by denomination, in York in 1901, 1935 and 1948 are less detailed, but illustrate changes in that city over almost half a century.

## Social and sanitary investigations

The growing interest in social and sanitary conditions in the 1830s and 1840s was stimulated partly by outbreaks of cholera and typhus in urban areas, which caused considerable alarm. Edwin Chadwick's *Report on the Sanitary Conditions of the Labouring Poor* to the Poor Law Commissioners in 1842 was a spur to the appointment of a Royal Commission into 'the State of Large Towns and Populous Districts' which reported in 1844 and 1845. The statistical societies presented evidence to these enquiries, the results of investigations which the societies had themselves carried out. The first such society was formed in Manchester in 1833 with the object of discussing 'subjects of political and social economy, and for the purpose of statistical inquiries'. Others were established in London in the following year, in Birmingham in 1835, Bristol in 1836 and Liverpool and Leeds, both in 1838. They were characteristic products of the enquiring and reforming climate of the 1830s; the British Association for the Advancement of Science held its first meeting in 1831 and the Statistical Office of the Board of Trade was formed in the following year. Enquiries into the social conditions of the period bore fruit most notably in J.R. McCulloch's *Statistical Account of the British Empire* (1837) and G.R. Porter's *Progress of the Nation* (1836–43), as well as in the reports and papers of the statistical societies. Changing membership and priorities led to the dissolution of the majority of the societies within a few years and only those in London and Manchester survived beyond the middle of the century. The Statistical Society of London became the Royal Statistical Society in 1887.

Detailed house-to-house investigations of the conditions of the working classes were prominent amongst the enquiries which these societies initiated. The Manchester Statistical Society investigated working-class districts in Manchester and the nearby towns of south-east Lancashire and also, in order to gain comparative evidence, produced a *Report on the Condition of the Working Classes in Kingston-upon-Hull* (1841), which was the result of a house-to-house survey by an 'intelligent agent' of the society. Hull had already been studied by that society as part of its enquiries into educational provision, which also generated reports on Manchester, Salford, Bury, Liverpool, Bolton and York between 1835 and 1840. These investigations into the state of education in urban areas produced figures for the numbers of schools and attendances at them, and some judgement of the quality of education available. They also contain information on the social conditions of the districts which had been studied. Indeed, one of the features of the statistical societies' reports and papers was the attempt to correlate the various elements which could be determined, in order to elucidate the conditions which were found in working-class areas. To do so they sought to collect detailed information. Birth and death rates, ages, the composition of families, the average ages of mothers, the numbers of houses, tenements and cellar dwellings, occupancy rates per room and per bed, countries of origin and the nature of employment were typical of the characteristics which were identified and could be tabulated. Attention was also turned to the domestic economy of the families which were interviewed, with incomes, rents, clothing, diet and standards of furnishing being investigated and categorized, albeit somewhat subjectively. The enquiries along these lines were not always very successful in obtaining hard evidence and some of the elements – on diet and incomes, for example – could not be ascertained in many households, so that the conclusions which were drawn were based on small samples. The author of a paper presented to the Manchester Statistical Society in 1889 on two working-class areas in Manchester and Salford divided the 4,440 residents who had occupations into three categories of very poor, poor and comfortable, but 34.5 per cent of the sample could not be classified. The societies covered many subjects, but public health and social issues remained in the forefront of their investigations. One-third of the papers read to the Manchester Statistical Society between 1853 and 1875 related to sanitary and poor law topics.[10]

The purpose of the statistical societies was not only to discover what the conditions of life in the urban areas were but also to disseminate their findings. To this end they published the reports submitted to them, in pamphlets, in their journals, or in both. For example, a report of a committee of the Statistical Society of London, on Church Lane in St Giles-in-the-Fields, was published in the society's *Journal* for 1848 and the society also ordered that 1,500 separate copies should be printed. A single volume of the London society's *Transactions* was published in 1837, becoming its quarterly *Journal* in the following year.[11] The Manchester Statistical Society's *Transactions* began in 1853, although many of its earlier papers and reports are extant. The publications of these two societies carried the results of the investigations conducted by the other statistical societies and neither confined itself to its own city or region. Indeed, the Statistical Society of London's interests had an international dimension.

The surge of interest in such social investigations which was characteristic of the 1830s and 1840s slackened somewhat thereafter, but was not entirely lost. Something of a revival may be identified in the establishment of the National Association for the Promotion of Social Science, which met annually between 1857 and 1886 and published its *Transactions*. Modelled to some extent on the British Association for the Advancement of Science, it divided its interests into sections, which included education, public health and 'social economy'.

Not all of the social enquiries were initiated by or reported to such societies. Many were published as individual pamphlets or books, designed to draw attention to social conditions in the Victorian cities. Among the investigations carried out in the late nineteenth century, two warrant a specific mention. Charles Booth's *Survey of the Life and Labour of the People in London* grew from a two volume first edition (1889–91), to nine volumes of a second edition (1892–7) and the 17 volumes of the third edition of 1902–3. It was based upon a massive amount of research, mostly collected during interviews. From this material Booth estimated the proportion of the population that lived in poverty and subdivided it into numerous social categories based upon a variety of indicators, but also drawing to some extent upon subjective criteria. His notebooks – which are in the British Library of Political and Economic Science at the London School of Economics – contain much information on the individuals who were interviewed and the conditions in which they lived, including notes on the state of their clothing and even some appraisal of their characters. Booth's work inspired Seebohm Rowntree to undertake an investigation of the living conditions of all the working classes in York in 1899, which involved a house-to-house survey of 11,560 families containing 46,754 people. Amongst the information which he collected, Rowntree established, or estimated where necessary, incomes and related them to the costs of a notional diet and domestic budget. From this data he developed the concept of the 'poverty line', distinguishing between what he regarded as 'primary' and 'secondary' poverty, calculating the proportion of the population that lived in poverty and identifying the causes. Rowntree published his findings in *Poverty: A Study of Town Life*

(1901) and his figures for the weekly wages of adult males were analysed by A.L. Bowley in a paper in the *Journal of the Royal Statistical Society* for 1902. Other work showed that York was a fairly typical town in respect of the proportion of the population living in poverty. In 1905 the Board of Trade conducted an investigation of wages, prices and rents in 89 large towns in the British Isles, 73 of them in England and Wales, presenting the results in the Parliamentary Papers for 1908, and it followed this up with a further survey in 1912.

The work of Booth and Rowntree was very influential and encouraged similar research with a strong quantitative element, although the reports of individual workers based upon personal observations continued to be produced. H. Llewellyn Smith, one of Booth's original researchers, supervised another investigation which was conducted along similar lines to those followed by his mentor. This was published between 1930 and 1935 as *The New Survey of London Life and Labour*, in nine volumes, two of which contain poverty maps. Rowntree himself carried out a second survey of York in 1936, which was published five years later as *Poverty and Progress: a Second Social Survey of York*, and a third, less satisfactory, one was undertaken in 1950. Rowntree was reluctant to take samples, but other researchers realised the validity of the results achieved from sampling and further refined the methodology of urban social surveys. In the early twentieth century there was great concern with the nature and causes of poverty. The recession between the two World Wars altered the nature of such investigations somewhat and there was then a growing interest in the effects of poverty, especially upon health. An investigation in Newcastle-upon-Tyne which was published in 1933 showed that one-third of schoolchildren who lived in the poorer parts of the city could be classified as unhealthy or in some way unfit. In 1931–4 the Medical Officer of Health for Stockton-on-Tees, G.C. M'Gonigle, carried out a survey of 800 families in which he investigated the relationship between malnutrition, death rates, poverty and social class. His findings were published in *Poverty and Public Health* (1936). During the same period Ernest Simon was conducting a survey of slum housing in Manchester, and Liverpool University was engaged on a wide-ranging enquiry into social conditions on Merseyside which it published in 1934 in three volumes as *The Social Survey of Merseyside*. These surveys were in the same tradition as those carried out a century before, although they were far more sophisticated than the earlier ones.

## The boards of health and the Local Government Board

One of the government's responses to the alarming cholera epidemic of 1831–2 was the compulsory creation of 800 local boards of health in England and Wales, acting initially under a central board and later under the Privy Council Office. Their functions overlapped those of the existing local bodies concerned with health and sanitary matters, and they were unpopular with ratepayers because of the extra expenditure which they created; they ceased to operate once the threat of the cholera outbreak had receded. Their papers should be found amongst local administrative records.

Chadwick's report of 1842 on sanitary conditions was followed up by propagandist associations, such as the Health of Towns Association, formed in 1844, which produced journals and other literature supporting his findings, and by the Royal Commission's reports of 1844 and 1845. This movement for the reform of health administration led to the passing of the 1848 Public Health Act. The Act established the General Board of Health, which generated a substantial body of evidence relating to the early-Victorian urban environment. This was contained in the reports of the Board's inspectors on the sanitary conditions in the districts which they investigated, and their enquiries also necessitated some examination of administrative arrangements. The reports include the recommendations of the inspectors, relevant correspondence and the evidence produced by their investigations, presented in the form of tabulated statistics and descriptive accounts of their fieldwork, which often included house-to-house inspections. The Board's inspector spent four days in Warwick, looking over the town and hearing evidence. His report recommended the installation of an adequate piped water supply, to replace the many wells which provided the town's drinking water, and a properly planned sewage system.[12] Warwick's death rate was 27 per 1,000 inhabitants, high enough for it to be inspected by the Board, which had powers to enquire into conditions in localities that had death rates in excess of 23 per 1,000, or which petitioned for the implementation of the 1848 Act. Local boards were established in those places which adopted the Act, or if the inspectors recommended such a step. By 1854 there were local boards in almost 200 towns, but London did not come within the General Board's jurisdiction. Reports on sanitary conditions were received by the local boards, which also generated minutes of their proceedings, accounts and other working papers. The reports to the General Board which were published between 1848 and 1857 comprised both the preliminary findings of the inspectors and the further investigations which may have followed from them. The British Library and the library of the Department of Health and Social Security have the most complete collections of such reports.

The General Board was disbanded in 1858. The local ones continued, without central direction, but with wider powers. They were required to submit annual reports to the Local Government Act Office at the Home Office. The Public Health Act of 1859 created a medical committee of the Privy Council, with a permanent medical officer. His influential annual reports did much to create the climate in which the 1866 Sanitary Act was passed, which standardized the powers of the local boards, removed the restrictions on their creation which had been imposed by the 1848 Act, made it obligatory for local authorities to implement regulations concerning the removal of nuisances, and added powers for the improvement or clearance of slums. In 1871 a single department covering public health matters, the Local Government Board, was created from the Poor Law Board, General Register Office, the Privy Council's Medical Committee and the Local Government Act Office. The Public Health Act of 1872 established the urban sanitary authorities and it was followed three years later by another, more wide ranging, Act. The 1872 Act constituted the municipal corporations as the urban sanitary authorities and they also took over the powers of the surviving bodies acting under local Improvement Acts. The Act also made the local boards of health, established in unincorporated towns and urban areas since 1848, the urban sanitary authorities. The records of the various bodies which were superseded under these Acts and the 1882 Municipal Corporations Act should have passed to their successor authorities.

The records of the various central boards are chiefly of an administrative nature; minutes, correspondence and related papers. These are held in the Ministry of Health classes of the Public Records at Kew. They are described in volume 96 of the List and Index Society's series. The *Annual Reports* of the Local Government Board summarize its operations and the information and statistics which it received from the local boards. They are also invaluable for providing the context for poor law and public health concerns in particular towns. The Board also received individual reports on the state of health of towns, especially those which were experiencing epidemics. An outbreak of scarlatina led to an investigation of Swindon in 1880 and the production of a 20–page report on the epidemic and the town's general sanitary condition. Typhoid fever prompted a report on Totnes in the following year and in 1883 the Board received reports from Taunton and Devonport because of the incidence of diphtheria in those towns. The reports were printed and are included in the Parliamentary Papers; separate copies may be held in local archives.

## Medical officers of health and sanitary inspectors

The first medical officer of health in England and Wales was appointed by the terms of Liverpool's Sanitary Act of 1846, and the 1848 Public Health Act allowed, but did not compel, local authorities to make similar appointments. By the Metropolis Local Management Act of 1855, which reorganized London's local government, all district boards of works and vestries in the capital were required to establish such a post and also appoint at least one inspector of nuisances. Medical officers of health, surveyors and inspectors of nuisances were appointed by the urban sanitary authorities constituted under the 1872 Public Health Act.

Birmingham's first full-time medical officer of health was appointed in that year and Coventry made a similar appointment two years later, but Exeter did not have even a part-time medical officer of health until 1894 and a full-time one was not appointed until 1914.[13]

These officers collected and analysed vital demographic information, identified those enumeration districts which had high death rates and tabulated the causes of death; they inspected bad housing and gave directions for its repair and cleansing, they supervised the cleaning of drains, the filling-in of cesspools and the removal of filth, and further attempted to reduce the risk of outbreaks of infectious disease by checking for adulterated foods and polluted water supplies and inspecting pig sties, slaughter houses and other premises where trades which were potential dangers to health were carried on. Domestic, commercial and industrial premises all came within their purview. They were not universally welcomed. In 1855 sanitary investigators who were collecting information in one of the less salubrious districts of St James's, Westminister were assailed by a 'fierce detachment of Irishmen' whose leader cried, 'I'll have no writing down in my place — I'll have no writing down in my place — not a divill amongst you shall write anything down here'. This was not the kind of response to encourage a detailed investigation. Yet information and statistics were gathered. In the following year an investigation of the Potteries area of North Kensington showed that the majority of its inhabitants obtained a living by rearing and fattening pigs; collecting refuse and offal, boiling it down and using the product for pig feed. The 1,041 pigs were narrowly outnumbered by the 1,147 people, who lived in 214 houses, which contained 595 rooms, at a density of 127 persons per acre.[14] This information is included in the medical officer of health's report and is not untypical of the kind of evidence which such reports contain.

The papers and correspondence of the medical officers of health should be found in the manuscript collections of the local authorities, and the officers' annual and occasional reports were commonly printed, either separately or as part of the authorities' reports. The Society of Medical Officers of Health's journal, *Public Health*, began publication in 1888, carrying articles on various aspects of the officers' work. The size of their reports to the local authorities, and the amount of detail which they carried, varied, reflecting the differing effectiveness and determination of the officers and perhaps, too, the responsiveness of their employers. Some officers were assiduous in gathering and analysing statistics and relating demographic factors to environmental ones, even including charts of rainfall and temperature readings in their reports. Such returns are useful in that the local registrars' figures are assembled and presented in a convenient form, and the accompanying explanatory statements and observations add an important extra dimension to the statistical evidence.

The attention of the inspectors and medical officers inevitably focused on the areas of overcrowded and inadequate housing and the conditions which that engendered. It was a part of their duties to report on housing, deemed to be unfit for habitation, that should be condemned and perhaps demolished under the slum clearance legislation which was passed from 1868 onwards. Their accounts of such areas are both descriptive and analytical, including details of the size, internal arrangements and condition of the houses, the sanitary provisions and the numbers of occupants. It was also necessary to conduct an enumeration of a district prior to the closure of the houses there, in order to gain some impression of the scale of the alternative accommodation which was required. The London County Council's clearance of the Boundary Street area of Shoreditch in the 1890s was preceded by a survey in which the numbers of inhabitants, houses and rooms were noted and the numbers of inhabitants per room and the cubic footage of space available to each occupant were tabulated. The numbers of employed adults and their occupations were also recorded.[15] Such an investigation provides a demographic and social profile of a district, but the areas dealt with in this way were generally relatively small and the characteristics which had attracted this kind of attention marked them out as not entirely typical examples of the urban environment. On the other hand, the identification of an area as a slum that should be cleared was related to the local authority's ability to carry out the work and perhaps provide alternative housing – this was not a requirement of the early slum clearance legislation – and so the areas surveyed and cleared may have been only marginally worse than others which could not receive similar attention for economic reasons.

## Poor relief

An indication of the size and identity of that section of the poor who, at some time in their lives, required formal assistance can be found in the records of the bodies which administered the Poor Law. The arrangements for providing aid for the poor evolved, through a series of measures, in the sixteenth, seventeenth and eighteenth centuries, and were completely overhauled by an Act of Parliament of 1834. Under the old Poor Law the parish was the unit for the administration of poor relief, although some borough councils directly involved themselves in its operation (p. 95). From the late seventeenth century, unions of parishes were created in a number of towns, either by private Acts of Parliament or by the terms of the general Acts of 1722 and 1782. The new Poor Law that was established by the 1834 Poor Law Amendment Act replaced the existing structure of poor relief based upon the parish, but not entirely so in those towns, such as Coventry, which already had a coherent system for dealing with the problem. The 1834 Act combined parishes compulsorily into unions, each of which was to have a workhouse for providing indoor relief. Administration was entrusted to an elected

Board of Guardians for each union. Central direction was provided by the Poor Law Commission until 1847, by its successor the Poor Law Board until 1871 and thereafter by the Local Government Board, which became part of the Ministry of Health in 1919. The arrangements instituted in 1834 remained more or less intact until 1929.

The records of the parish officers in charge of the operation of the Poor Law, the overseers of the poor, include accounts, settlement certificates, examinations, removal orders and inventories of paupers' goods, which give insights into the identities and to some extent the lives of the poor. From the accounts of payments to the needy the pattern of relief, both individually and collectively, can be traced. The operation of the old Poor Law in the early nineteenth century is illustrated in the replies to the questionnaire distributed in 1832 to sample parishes by the Poor Law Commissioners, under the heading 'Answers to Town Queries'. This bulky evidence was printed in the volumes of the Commissioners' *Report*.

The administrative records generated by the Boards of Guardians consist essentially of minutes of their meetings, accounts and correspondence. Information on individuals who fell within the purview of the system can be gleaned from such material, but other records that were produced by its operation are more illuminating on the extent and nature of poverty in a town. Registers of paupers receiving relief should have been kept from 1691, but may not survive from such an early date or in long series. They are invaluable in tracing the incidence of relief, for they typically note the name, sex, age, marital status, address and trade of each person and also the reasons why assistance was required. Groupings by these characteristics should provide a profile of the urban poor, their backgrounds and places of residence. Other registers in which individuals can be traced include those listing admissions to and discharges from the workhouse, the births and deaths of its residents and the apprenticeship of poor youths. Relief orders, the application and report books of the staff, and the financial accounts of its operations give an indication of the changing scale and cost of poor relief, the nature of the workhouse – some came to be used largely as hospitals or orphanages – and of life within it. The union has to be the unit of study when using such records, which do not distinguish individuals, for the aggregate figures and other data which they contain cannot be divided amongst the component parishes. This can be a problem, for all except the largest towns were amalgamated in unions with neighbouring rural parishes, in which the patterns of poverty differed from those in urban areas.

Parish, borough and quarter sessions records should contain the material generated under the old Poor Law, and those of the guardians should have passed to the successor local government authorities and perhaps thence to the appropriate record office. Other records were produced by the communications which passed between the unions and the three successive central authorities responsible for Poor Law matters.

They are dominated by the 16,741 volumes for the period 1834–1900 which are in class M.H. 12 at the Public Record Office at Kew. The material is arranged alphabetically by union under counties and the vast majority of it consists of correspondence. Much of the correspondence may duplicate the copies which the unions kept in their own letter books, although the survival of such books has not been particularly good. Indeed, the series in M.H. 12 are not complete and none from after 1900 have survived.

The formal Poor Law arrangements were supplemented by the work of various charitable bodies, such as the expressively named Soup Charity in Manchester. In 1869 the Charity Organisation Society was founded, with the aim of co-ordinating the various efforts of the poor relief organizations and directing assistance to those it regarded as the deserving poor, thus overcoming the problems which were thought to arise through the indiscriminate distribution of charity. Its operations were based upon a system of casework in which the circumstances of those seeking relief were investigated in some detail, a process which included interviews with the applicants and visits by the society's district case workers. The findings of the investigations were kept in a series of forms and record books. The procedure generated a great deal of material relating to employment and wages, indebtedness and the structure of credit, standards of living, household composition and the general condition of the urban poor who came to the society's attention. The files of case histories are a rich source and may have been deposited in local record offices, albeit with some restrictions of access because of considerations of confidentiality. Some files have been destroyed, including those for London.[16] The society produced other, more immediately digestible, evidence through its efforts to publicize its activities and attract subscribers. Conscious of the benefits of publicity, it placed advertisements requesting help for typical families or individuals, describing their circumstances in some detail and outlining the reasons for the need for relief. The *Charity Organisation Reporter* was a weekly which ran from 1872 until replaced in 1885 by the monthly *Charity Organisation Review*. The society also published pamphlets and tracts, some of which were issued in the collected *Charity Organisation Papers* (1881, 1896) and it also produced four series of *Occasional Papers*, published between 1896 and 1907. The other major source produced by the society was its *Annual Reports*, both those which were issued by the society's council and those of the district committees, which were published separately. Like the *Reporter* and the *Review*, the *Annual Reports* carried numerous case histories and articles, as well as summaries of the work of the society over the previous year. Such material provides uneven coverage, for the society was not established in all urban areas and was not equally successful in those in which it was active. Nevertheless, the way in which the Charity Organisation Society sought to implement its policies, and the manner in which it disseminated its findings, created an important body of evidence on the reasons for poverty as well as giving insights into the lives of the poor in late Victorian and Edwardian cities and towns.

# Chapter Six
# CIVIC ADMINISTRATION

## Charters and Improvement Acts

The constitutional arrangements of the cities and incorporated boroughs are set out in their charters, which established their legal and administrative status on a separate footing from that of the counties. Many charters issued in the twelfth and thirteenth centuries were private grants by the lord, not by the crown, but thereafter the crown was invariably the grantor. A few towns did not obtain a royal confirmation and their rights remained based upon a private grant. This was the case at Tetbury, Gloucestershire, where the inhabitants actually bought out the lord's rights in the seventeenth century and transferred them to a body of seven feoffees.[1] In the majority of cases, however, a royal charter was obtained. Between 1066 and 1660 more than 320 English and Welsh towns received a charter, although it should be added that some of those which thereby acquired the legal basis of a town did not achieve any other degree of urbanization, or had declined to such an extent that they were not at all urban by the beginning of the sixteenth century. Others received several grants and confirmations; 12 were bestowed upon Doncaster between 1194 and 1688.[2] Some grants made only minor modifications to existing arrangements, reiterating existing privileges and perhaps ironing out some anomalies which had become apparent since the previous charter was issued. Other charters made major constitutional changes. The two volumes of *British Borough Charters* edited by Adolphus Ballard and James Tait (1913 and 1923) note those charters which were issued between 1042 and 1307. *British Borough Charters 1307–1660*, edited by Martin Weinbaum (1943), provides a list and an analysis, and includes summaries of the more significant grants of incorporation.

The procedure for obtaining a charter during the early modern period contained a number of distinct stages.[3] Perhaps the most informative documents which it generated are the petitions to the crown that initiated the process, and set out the petitioners' requirements, and the reports on those petitions which were prepared by law officers or other officials. A number of other stages followed before the charter was issued and entered on the charter rolls, which ceased to be used in 1516, or the patent rolls. The charter rolls are calendared to 1516 and there is a similar series of *Calendars* for the patent rolls up to 1558, although for the reign of Henry VIII their contents are included in the *Letters and Papers*. The patent rolls constitute class C 66 in the Public Record Office at Chancery Lane. They include grants of incorporation to such organizations as guild companies and the governing bodies of schools, as well as borough charters. The petitions and reports are to be found in the records of the State Paper Office and in the Privy Council's papers, which survive only from 1698. Some relevant material for the nineteenth century is in the Home Office records. The State Papers are calendared to 1704 and the Privy Council papers, class PC 1, are listed in volumes 24, 35 and 36 of the List and Index series.

Amongst such records are petitions and submissions, not only requesting incorporation and providing evidence in support of a request but also opposing it. In 1864 separate petitions against the proposed incorporation of Southport were presented to the Privy Council by householders and property owners in the town, Justices of the Peace, a majority of the Commissioners acting under an Improvement Act of 1846, and the lords of the manor of North Mcols, of which the town was a part.[4] Nevertheless, a charter was granted two years later. Such material also includes maps of the area of a proposed borough, papers arguing the case for its extent – whether to include the suburbs and nearby places – and reports on the merits of a case.

Charters specify the date on which the grant became operative and the title of the corporation, giving it the legal status to sue and to be sued by the name of the corporation. They also define the area of jurisdiction. This was commonly not much beyond the built-up area, although at Bristol and York it covered a larger tract, and two hundreds of Gloucestershire were annexed to the corporation of Gloucester by its charter of 1483, an arrangement which continued until 1662.[5] Where a town subsequently spilled over its boundaries, such suburbs lay beyond the corporation's control. Among other grants to a corporation typically included in its charters were a common seal, the power to hold land, the authority to make self-governing ordinances and to enforce them within its own courts, the right of perpetual succession and the power to elect its own officers. The offices were specified and their first holders named; the composition of the common council, with the method of selection to it, was described and the transition from the outgoing constitution to the new one was usually provided for in some detail. The trading rights were an important element of the charters, allowing the burgesses the privilege of trading within the town free of tolls, and granting or confirming weekly markets and periodic fairs and the right to levy tolls. The various other miscellaneous rights and privileges included can be taken to reflect the current concerns or ambitions of the corporation, for they were inserted in response to the petitions of the inhabitants, not at the instance of the crown. Indeed, charters could incorporate whatever clauses the inhabitants wished, so long, of course, as their requests did not run counter to royal policy or offend a stronger interest which could successfully resist their petition. The constitutional organization described in a charter does not invariably present a complete picture of the situation, for there may have been some customary arrangements which remained unaffected by the issue of a charter. None of the early modern charters granted to Bewdley refer to the two bridgewardens, who, in the seventeenth century at least, collected and disbursed the town's revenues.[6] Nor were the charters' terms inviolable, for experience and changed circumstances may have produced some modifications which came to be tacitly accepted.

Charters are often beautifully executed documents, among the finest examples of penmanship of their respective periods. They were highly prized as the basis of a corporation's privileges and legal standing and so were carefully preserved, however cavalierly other categories of documents may have been treated. For the same reason, they have received considerable attention from antiquarians and local historians and many are in print, either in full or in summary, in local histories or in separate editions, making them readily accessible.

The *First Report* of the Royal Commission investigating the municipal corporations in England and Wales (1835) contains a summary of the constitutional and administrative arrangements of 183 such corporations, set out, in the appendix, in tabular form. It typically lists the charters granted to the city or borough, identifying the operative one, and the relevant private Acts of Parliament. It also itemizes the officers, describing their selection and functions, notes the size of the aldermanate and common council and defines the qualifications required for entering the freedom. A summary of the financial position is included, with the revenue and expenditure broken down into categories, and the jurisdiction of those courts held within the city or borough is described. The *Report* also contains the evidence taken by the commissioners from the officers of some towns which establishes, often in considerable detail, the operational practicalities of administration. The *Report* is, therefore, a useful source for the organization of borough administration in the early nineteenth century and a summary of the constitutional arrangements that had applied since the grant of the governing charter, which in many towns was a late seventeenth-century one.

The arrangements within the unincorporated towns often have to be established from the surviving administrative records themselves, whether of the town's court of record, a manorial court leet, or the parish records. It is unusual to have a clear statement of their organization, unless this was made in relation to a dispute over jurisdictions within the town. The acquisition of Improvement Acts in the late eighteenth and nineteenth centuries established such administration upon a more clearly regulated footing.[7] The records of the Trustees or Commissioners empowered by such Acts are commonly amongst those of the successor bodies who superseded them by the terms of the nineteenth-century local government reforms.

The earliest such local Act for the parishes in the metropolis was the Watch Act for Westminster and Hanover Square, 1735, and the following century or so saw the passing of a veritable plethora of Acts for the London parishes, and others granted for virtually every sizeable provincial city or town, both incorporated and unincorporated. Policing was the subject of many Acts, and other matters covered were the paving, cleansing and lighting of the streets, the provision of water supplies and sewage and refuse disposal. They were commonly drafted by those who were then empowered to enforce them. The earliest ones created 'closed' commissions with a co-opted membership, but the later ones tended to provide for the election of their members. The passing of such Acts for incorporated cities and towns led to some overlapping of jurisdictions, and it is advisable to establish the parameters of the responsibilities of those implementing such Acts and the functions which were exercised by the corporation.

## Minutes of proceedings

The process of administration generated a number of series of records, the central one amongst them being the minutes of the meetings of the administering body. These are generally substantial and detailed, covering virtually all of the business which was handled, perhaps indexed at some stage by a town clerk or an interested antiquarian, although such indices should be regarded as a guide and not relied upon as being wholly accurate or comprehensive. A series of minutes was usually begun once a charter or Improvement Act became operative and a new volume may have been started when a new charter or Act was obtained, or, after the reforms of the 1830s, as a kind of symbolic new beginning. The increasing responsibilities assumed by local authorities and the requirements placed upon them by government legislation are reflected in the greater bulk of their minutes, especially from the early nineteenth century onwards. A nineteenth-century development was the printing of the minutes, a consequence of the public accountability required by the reforms of civic government; it was compulsory for the councils of the boroughs incorporated by the 1835 Municipal Corporations Act to print their minutes of proceedings. This makes such material easier to use, but a trend to greater formality – and perhaps some loss of detail – in their presentation may also be detected. The regular coverage of council meetings in the local press does something to offset this tendency, for the newspapers' reports typically include members' statements and information that was not minuted. They may also give an indication of the mood of a meeting, which cannot always be sensed from the formal record, and they are an invaluable guide to the operation of councils during the period when political parties became established in urban government. There was also a growing tendency for the council meetings to receive and decide upon the reports of the standing and special committees which came to deal with the detailed business of the corporation. The committees covered a range of routine and occasional matters and their numbers grew as the work load expanded and became more diverse. Their reports are commonly entered in the volumes of the council minutes, but the records of their own meetings were maintained separately and may survive as further series which should be consulted for the extra detail which they contain. During the late nineteenth century it became customary for many councils to issue annual reports describing their work over the previous year. These are unlikely to add information to that available from the minutes, but they are generally a convenient summary of the council's work and perhaps include a clear declaration of policy on current concerns.

Related series of records may include the agendas for the council's meetings, the rough minutes taken at them, from which the fair copy was later written up, and the chronicle of the deliberations of an inner body, such as the mayor's council at Oxford. Examination of the records themselves will indicate the relative importance of the meetings of the full council and those of any smaller group of this kind, and perhaps show the extent to which issues were discussed by the inner body before they came before the council. The town clerk was the chief administrative officer of an incorporated town and his notebooks normally carry information which can be used to supplement the more formal record regarding, for example, the council's membership and the votes cast at its meetings.

Other minutes which may survive are those of the various bodies which dealt with particular aspects of urban administration but were not under the control of the corporation. This applies to those of the Boards of Guardians created by the Poor Law Amendment Act of 1834, which themselves may have spawned subsidiary series, and those of the district Boards of Health. Minutes of the meetings of the governing bodies of the guilds and livery companies may also exist. Such organizations were chiefly concerned with the regulation of their membership and of the trade, management of their property, and the disbursement of funds allocated or bequeathed for charitable purposes for the benefit of members of the company or their dependants. Their records may also include ordinances, accounts, rentals, enrolments of leases and registers of apprentices and members. The size and relative importance of a company may be gauged from such minutes and the overlap between its leading figures and those of the corporation's own council can also be examined.

## The contents of the minutes

Although the contents of the councils' minutes are by no means standard, some common themes may be indicated. The meetings may have followed an identifiable pattern which shows the structure of the civic year, the monthly or weekly frequency of assemblies and perhaps a preference for convening on particular days of the week. Changes to such a pattern may indicate a response to a crisis, with meetings held more often than was usual and on days which were not commonly employed. The civic year was centred on the annual elections of the officers and the minutes typically begin the new year with a list of such officers, both honorary and functional, perhaps including all members of the council. The more senior posts required quite a bit of time and attention and could be considered as rather onerous, leading to refusals to serve. Such refusals were likely to be more frequent at times of crisis, but they perhaps also reflect a decline in the regard with which high civic office was held. Those who refused to serve in an office to which they had been chosen or which their senority required them to fill were liable to a fine. This may have been waived if their reasons were thought to be valid, but on the other hand it was enforced in many cases, if only to act as a deterrent to others who may also have wished to avoid holding office. Indeed, the size of the fine tends to indicate the extent of refusals and the consequent degree of exasperation of the council. The death of officers within their year of office and the choice of replacements are noted in the minutes. A reasonably comprehensive list of the holders of the various offices can be compiled from this evidence. If there is a gap in the surviving minutes, then this information can be obtained from oath rolls, which record the taking of the oaths required on admission to an office. From the early eighteenth century, announcements in newspapers provide a further alternative source. For instance, *The London Daily Post* for 23 September 1735 carried the announcement that John Neale, 'an eminent Apothecary in St Albans', had been chosen mayor of that town two days earlier.

It may not be easy to establish the dates of membership for all councillors, at least for the early modern period, for new admissions and departures were not always minuted and, unless those present were noted in the minutes for every meeting, only an annual list of members may be available. There is, too, the perennial problem of identifying with absolute certainty those councillors who had a fairly common name and were not given any further distinguishing description, such as their trade, or the appellation of 'senior' or 'junior'. Such considerations do not apply for the modern period or, indeed, for many earlier sets of minutes, in which case the careers of individual members can be traced, from first admission, to promotion to an inner council, if appropriate, the aldermanate and perhaps other offices. The development of standing committees required the attendance of council members who were willing and able to attend to their business and it should be possible to discover the frequency of individuals' appearances at their meetings. The size and composition of the group which was active in civic administration can be identified, from which it may emerge that a particular trade or interest, or group of families, formed a dominant element. One half of the Elizabethan mayors of Norwich were grocers and the Merchant Adventurers were the predominant clique at Newcastle-upon-Tyne.[8]

A council's concern to regulate admissions to the freedom of the corporation should be reflected in the minutes, with occasional notes of the names of those who were admitted by patrimony or after serving an apprenticeship, which may be used as a check for the freemen and apprentices' registers, or as a substitute, if such registers are not extant (pp. 65–6). Matters arising from the procedure of admission by apprenticeship also came before the council, such as maltreatment, desertion, or false declarations as to the length of time served. Such information is commonly to be found in some quantity in the minutes of the guild companies and the records of the civic courts. All of the freedoms granted by council act should, by definition, be mentioned in the minutes, with the size of the fee, if one was levied. Such fees could be a useful supplement to a corporation's income and an unusually large number of admissions by fine may be related to its financial problems or a particular need. In order to cover the cost of obtaining its charter of 1586, Shrewsbury granted its freedom to 20 new burgesses at a fee of £5 each.[9] Freemen admissions by council act also have to be seen in terms of patterns of patronage and politics. There was commonly an increase of registrations and grants of freedom shortly before parliamentary elections.

A related matter was the operation of the market and the trading arrangements within the town, together with the protection of privileges. This consisted of the periodic restatement of the terms on which trading could take place and an emphasis of the regulations against foreigners, that is non-freemen, operating within the borough. Such reiteration of rights granted by charter may reflect an awareness that they had been allowed to lapse to an unacceptable degree and that they should be more rigorously enforced. This was the case in many towns from time to time and especially after the disruptions of the Civil War. At Oxford the council noted in 1646 that 'divers strangers and others, which are not freemen of this Citie' were trading there as if they were entitled to do so and it ordered that their shops should be closed down.[10] Such trading restrictions declined in importance and effectiveness from the late seventeenth century and the controls gradually lapsed. Council concern with them similarly decreased, although the voting rights held by freemen were still carefully supervised.

A council was usually involved with property in two ways; in the construction and management of public buildings and in the leasing of its own buildings and lands and those which it managed on behalf of charities. The various stages in the erection of public buildings can usually be traced from the minutes (p. 41). Mention of the granting of a lease is commonly limited to a bare statement of the identity of the property, the name of the lessee and the terms of the grant. The leases themselves are clearly the more informative source (pp. 35–6). The entries in the minutes can be used to trace the extent to which council members, especially the senior ones, took leases of corporation property on favourable terms, a practice which seems to have been accepted, in the early modern period at least, as a legitimate perquisite for civic office holders. Roughly two-thirds of leases granted by Worcester corporation in 1617–36 went to council members and some of the remainder to their widows or relatives. In 1624 Lincoln council minutes recorded an order restricting the number of leases that could be held by council members, which was related to their seniority.[11] Minutes of proceedings also note a corporation's purchase of property and the purpose for which it was acquired. They may include extracts of the appropriate sections of the wills of those who had made bequests to the corporation or to one of the charities which it administered.

A common arrangement was that a corporation was responsible for the money donated for charitable purposes, such as the care of orphans or to apprentice poor children. It was also necessary to make provision for the adult poor and others who were, perhaps temporarily, in need because of a crisis such as an outbreak of plague or a period of dearth and consequent high prices. Management of a pesthouse, in times of epidemic, and of almshouses and hospitals, was also a civic responsibility. Related concerns included the provision of water supplies, control of the market, the removal of refuse and the disposal of sewage. Care was also needed in regulating particularly noxious trades that may have been a hazard to health, such as tanning and soap boiling, and in reducing the risk of fire by imposing controls on building materials and dangerous premises. These aspects of the urban milieu led to the promulgation and enforcement of by-laws, noted in council minutes and perhaps separately printed for circulation. It was partly due to the growing neglect of such matters by the governing bodies of many towns in the eighteenth century that local Improvement Acts were obtained. The reforms of the next century brought most aspects of urban life back under direct civic control, including the oversight of such utilities as gas and electricity supplies, which were originally in private hands, and led to the creation of, for example, municipal fire brigades. Health care and sanitation also became primary responsibilities. Education, too, was a feature of urban life which involved civic interests throughout the early modern and modern periods, becoming increasingly prominent following the relevant Acts of Parliament of the late nineteenth and early twentieth centuries. On the other hand, the establishment in 1853 of the Charity Commission removed the administration of charities from the corporations.

Other matters diminished in importance during the four centuries under review. Admission to the freedom came to be of purely honorary significance and its relevance in terms of voting rights disappeared with electoral reform and the extension of the franchise. The need to maintain a civic armoury was another common concern of the early modern era which gradually declined. Such armouries could be considerable; that in Northampton town hall in 1661 contained 149 muskets, two blunder-busses, 30 swords, various pieces of armour and a great deal of ammunition, including seven hand grenades.[12] Religious affairs also loomed larger then than they were later to do, for councils were actively involved in that sphere, appointing lecturers and, not infrequently, becoming embroiled in disputes with the ecclesiastical authorities.

One perennial factor which exercised the minds and abilities of councillors, to a greater or lesser degree, was finance. Financial records are discussed below, but related matters and the decisions which they involved do appear among the entries in the minutes. The routine aspects of income and expenditure did not normally require a council's attention, indeed the majority of financial matters that were minuted were the unusual or occasional ones. Sanction was required for buying equipment, spending on the erection, repair and general maintenance of buildings, for charitable payments to assist individuals, and donations to other com-munities in emergencies or in response to appeals for specific purposes that were thought to be worthy. Payments for civic entertainments had to be approved, or queried, as did the arrangements for the visits of royalty or dignitaries and the expense which they engendered. Exceptional expendi-ture, or perhaps slowly accumulated deficit, was covered by borrowing or raising extraordinary revenue by the levy of an extra rate. Such decisions to increase income, and perhaps the mechanics of how it should be done – such as who the assessors of a rate were to be – had to come before the council and so are generally recorded in its minutes. This may also apply to the raising of taxes for central government, although that process did not necessarily involve a council directly.

Correspondence with and directions from government form part of a category of council business which may be described as external relations. This also included consideration of the choice of members of Parliament and communications with them while Parliament was in session. Powerful patrons and a borough's recorder may also have been requested to keep an eye on its interests in the formulation of policy and the drafting of legislation. The claims of patrons and local magnates had to be taken into account and, when necessary, reconciled as far as possible. Some legal disputes which arose were the result of threats, real or anticipated, to a town's rights or prosperity. These may have involved an issue such as riparian rights. Beverley corporation kept a jealous eye on the navigation of the River Hull, which involved it in a long-running dispute with the town of Hull and prompted it to investigate the effects of the proposed drainage schemes for the nearby carr lands at the end of the eighteenth century.[13] Another subject which attracted attention was the apparent infringement of a town's privileges by those held by or granted to another town close by. The Elizabethan corporation of Newcastle-upon-Tyne tried assiduously to get the liberties of the Bishop of Durham's town of

Gateshead withdrawn.[14] Not all communications with other towns were of a contentious nature, however, for there was a great deal of co-operation on matters of mutual interest, and also exchanges of information. From 1855 the London vestries and district boards of works had to deal with the Metropolitan Board of Works and, from 1889, its successor, the London County Council.

## Letters and petitions

Letters and petitions formed a significant part of the mass of working papers generated by urban administration. Correspondence was necessarily exchanged with government and other communities in the conduct of a town's external relations, but it was also generated by transactions with, for example, tenants, householders and contractors carrying out work for the council. Their contents cover the whole range of urban administration, but many of them contain requests of various kinds. Such applications were presented in a more formal manner in petitions. Petitions were submitted to a town council by individuals or groups within the town and they, and the council itself, could also be petitioners to central government. A petitioning group could be a formal one representing a specific interest or a body such as a guild company, or an informal one which had come together to make a request on a particular point. This indicates a major consideration in the interpretation of such material, for a petition may have been drafted by or for a person or caucus expressing an unrepresentative, or misleading, point of view, or with a distortion or exaggeration of the circumstances in order to obtain assistance or redress. A counter-petition may have given another slant on a case. In 1684 a number of the parishioners of the Oxford suburb of St Clement's petitioned the crown that the parish be incorporated within the city, while a smaller group, apparently led by the rector, presented a petition requesting that this should not be done.[15] One petition is amongst the council's records and the other in the state papers for Charles II's reign, but both survive, whereas in many cases one such petition may be missing and so the impression gained is distorted. Identification of the signatories of petitions and letters helps in their interpretation. Of course, not all requests were biased, contentious or misleading and many were straightforward applications for specific benefits, such as admission to the freedom or the granting of a lease.

The survival of such loose papers in local records has been patchy, to say the least. The low value placed upon them once the case had been dealt with and the increasing pressure on storage space in many town halls often resulted in their destruction. This was not invariably the case. At Leicester a selection of loose papers made in the mid nineteenth century was bound, together with the draft council minutes, as a series designated 'Hall Papers Bound' and covering the period 1583–1709. Complete categories of papers have been preserved as being of especial importance or simply through being designated as being in some way separate. The government papers sent to Rye during the nineteenth century constitute a category of this kind.[16] The material generated by standing or special committees may also have survived intact, having a natural coherence. Even if the original papers have been destroyed, copies may exist in other sources. Such material was entered in the council minutes themselves in some towns, in summary or in full, although this does not seem to have been a particularly common practice. Some town clerks kept letter books in which both outgoing and incoming correspondence was entered, and the survival rate of such volumes far exceeds that of bundles of loose papers.

## Civic accounts

Supervision of a corporation's finances was entrusted to those council members who held the post of treasurer, commonly for one or two years each. Their annual accounts were inspected by an audit committee. The treasurers were given different titles in different towns, but a common designation was that of chamberlain. The simplest arrangement was that one or more treasurers dealt with all of the civic finances and rendered a single account annually. In some boroughs the responsibility was divided between two or more sets of officers, who handled separate accounts. At Oxford, the chamberlains, the original financial officers, were supplemented in 1448 by the keykeepers and thereafter both sets of officers collected and disbursed funds and prepared accounts. Their responsibilities were demarcated, although in practice the division between them was often blurred. The functions of some posts were gradually lost and eventually appointments to such offices were discontinued. The finances managed by the wardens of town houses in Banbury were taken over at the turn of the seventeenth century by the bridgemasters and they, the mayor and the chamberlains all rendered separate accounts. At Hull the town's husbands, took over the civic finances during the eighteenth century, although they nominally remained the responsibility of the chamberlains, who neither handled the finances nor prepared the accounts which were submitted in their names.[17] The surviving records should reflect the changes in the administrative arrangements for dealing with the finances, but they may, as at Hull, largely conceal them. Because of such changes, the study of a corporation's finances over a period of time may require the investigation of a number of different, and evolving, series of accounts.

The typical early modern treasurers' accounts are divided into their 'charge' and 'discharge', that is, revenue and expenditure, with both elements separated into their component parts. The balance at the end of the year shows the sum owed either by the treasurers to the corporation or to them by the corporation; this surplus or deficit was then carried forward to the following year's account. This form of single entry book-keeping was derived from that of the medieval *compotus* and, although some corporations' finances became quite complex, it continued to be used into the modern period in many boroughs, before it was superseded by double entry book-keeping.

Revenue included income from the corporation's property. The rents received during the year of account were entered, with a distinction made between those which were due in that year and arrears from previous years. A full rental may be presented in the account. Rents were also received for such items as purprestures – building encoachments on the public streets – dunghills and market stalls. Tolls from markets and fairs and fines for breaches of the regulations governing their operation produced further income. In 1832–3 the tolls of the markets and six annual fairs, with the rent for the house in the market place, brought in 36 per cent of Hereford corporation's income. Bridge tolls formed a similar, but generally small, income at some towns. Quay dues were taken at most ports and the entries of such sums may, as at Newcastle-upon-Tyne, include details of the vessels for which the dues were paid.[18] Gloucester corporation rented out the cranes at the quayside. Fines taken at the granting or renewal of leases of corporation lands and houses formed another, and often considerable, item of revenue from property. In 1663–4 such fines produced 14 per cent of Gloucester corporation's revenue, while rents and arrears received generated just over a half of it.[19] Some corporations chose to maintain rents at their existing levels while taking increasingly larger fines for granting new or renewed leases. Examination of the balance between rents and fines may indicate whether such a policy was being pursued and the extent to which it altered the nature of the income received from property.

Fee income was a second major element of corporation revenues. Fees were received from those who became freemen, by patrimony, apprenticeship and council act, and for the enrolments of new apprentices (pp. 65–6). At Oxford and Gloucester, fines for admission to the freedom included sums contributed to a bucket fund, intended for the purchase of leather fire buckets. Other fees were taken from new members of common councils, those who were raised to the aldermanate, and sometimes from those who resigned as councillors. The sums received for such fees fluctuated, depending on the stability of council membership. Between 1623 and 1640 those taken from new admissions to the two chambers of Worcester's common council produced, on average, a little over £4 each year, at a time when annual income was almost £300.[20] Levies were also commonly taken from office holders, from those who actually served in an office, often supposedly in lieu of giving a feast for the other councillors, and also from those who paid a fine in order to be excused from service. These were potentially quite productive. The typical levy taken by London corporation in the late sixteenth century from those who were excused from serving as sheriff was £200.[21] The chamberlains at York in the eighteenth century each paid £6 13s. 4d. exoneration money, ostensibly for not serving in offices which were actually defunct, and the corporation there also took a fee from those who wished to avoid an office, notably that of sheriff, which was £100 in the 1700s and twice that sum by the 1780s. In 1750 the corporation received £50 exoneration money and £418 for freemen's admissions, out of a total income of £1,495.[22]

Miscellaneous income included fines taken by the civic courts for breaches of the by-laws and for such things as the release of impounded livestock. Sales of surplus materials and various other items also added small sums to revenues. In the 1650s Gloucester corporation occasionally sold timber, tile, stone and pebble and in 1655–6 received £2 for some millstones and, rather more curiously, 1s 0d for just one 'seat door out of Trinity Church'.[23] Gifts and bequests were received from time to time, usually for specific purposes. More regular income was represented by the interest from investments, which became of some importance in the eighteenth and nineteenth centuries as borough corporations put surplus funds into canal, turnpike and railway companies, or into government stock.

It was sometimes necessary to raise extra income to cover immediate large-scale expenditure or to reduce or clear an accumulated deficit. This was normally done by levying a rate or by loans. In early seventeenth-century Worcester a rate of this kind, known as a fifteenth, brought in almost £18, but the corporation was not restricted to collecting a single fifteenth at any one time, hence double, treble or fourfold fifteenths were ordered, according to the exigencies of the moment. On the other hand, although Banbury corporation undoubtedly had the authority to levy such a rate, it preferred to find extraordinary income by raising loans and occasionally by more informal means, such as taking contributions from members of the common council.[24] The amounts received from rates of this kind should appear in the regular accounts, with arrears from earlier collections entered separately. It should be possible to glean considerable information from the entries relating to loans, for the individuals from whom a corporation borrowed are usually named in the accounts and can be identified, as common councillors, other prominent citizens, or perhaps people from the surrounding countryside or another town. Charitable funds administered by a corporation were also a source of loans. As the scale and complexity of civic finances increased with the widening of administrative responsibility during the nineteenth and twentieth centuries, so did the size and duration of loans. The sources of such funds shifted from individuals to central government and to the financial market, with banks and insurance companies as prominent lenders. The nature of the rate also changed, becoming a regular, rather

than occasional, source of revenue. Improvement Acts typically authorized the levy of a rate for specific purposes, such as the paving and lighting
of the streets. General rates, although allowed by legislation of 1739– 40,
were only gradually adopted in the second half of the eighteenth and the
nineteenth centuries. Not until the Rating and Valuation Act of 1925
were the various rates for separate purposes superseded by a single rate.
The changing balance between the various components of civic revenue
can be traced from the accounts.

The section of the accounts for the treasurers' discharge, or expenditure, was usually organized in a similar form to that for revenue; that is,
with payments grouped by category and perhaps with a section at the end
of the standard groupings for the miscellaneous, non-recurrent, items.
Such an arrangement was not adopted for all civic accounts, however,
and payments may not be subdivided but simply entered in an unbroken
sequence. Dating of the items of expenditure may be difficult, for many
treasurers did not date the individual entries. Even in those accounts in
which the entries are in a single sequence, there is no certainty that they
were entered in strict order of payment and that the sequence was a
chronological one. In this respect the rough preliminary accounts may be
more helpful and the actual vouchers on which payment was made should
provide even fuller information, both in terms of dates and of greater
detail on the nature of the payment and the creditor. The survival of such
rough accounts and vouchers has not been good, however. It was
probably a common practice to dispose of them once the audit of the
year's accounts was completed.

The categories of payments broadly reflected the nature of civic
administration, which has been considered in connection with the
minutes of councils' proceedings. Salaries and allowances were a major
item, listing payments to those employed by the corporation, from its
recorder to the street sweepers. In mid-eighteenth-century York there
were 50 or so recipients of such fees and wages.[25] Related items included
the purchase of gowns, uniforms and staves of office. Payments were also
recorded for wages to those undertaking casual work on such tasks as
paving, building or the clearance of snow and ice. Public works
represented another important category, including the maintenance and
furnishing of the corporation's buildings, perhaps with the accounts for
the erection of a new building entered in a separate section. Street
maintenance, cleaning and lighting, the upkeep of bridges, quays and
harbour works and, for much of the early modern period, the repair of
town walls and gates, made other calls upon the civic purse. Entries for the
costs of laying out new streets provide evidence for the expansion of the
built-up area, with payments for the drawing of the necessary plans and
the measuring and staking out of the land. A further category of
outgoings related to property was that for rents paid by the corporation,
including the fee farm rents payable to the crown. Legal costs, for

property transactions and other business, formed another element of civic expenditure, and a variable one, depending upon the amount of litigation in which the corporation was engaged. The interest on loans and the repayment of borrowed capital also had to be met by the civic treasurers. Costs were also incurred in the provision of justice, with payments for the patrolling of the streets, the maintenance and administration of a gaol, the furnishing of instruments of punishment – stocks, pillory and gallows – and the oversight of prisoners. The entertainment of the judges at the assizes and the justices at the quarter sessions were further items to be discharged out of a corporation's revenues. In 1663–4 the expense of lodgings for the judges who presided at the assizes in Gloucester cost the corporation there £8 and a salmon, two lamprey pies, a sheep and a lamb, two dozen pigeons, nine partridges and unspecified numbers of turkeys, geese and chickens for their delectation accounted for a further £6 3s. 6d.[26] In the eighteenth century the assizes and quarter sessions became increasingly important dates in the social calendar. Yet they were only a part of the round of regular feasts and festivities which punctuated the civic year and formed a fairly substantial category of expenditure in many towns. Dinners and entertainments were also laid on for such occasional events as the receipt of a new charter, the visit of a dignitary, and national celebrations for a coronation, a victorious battle or the conclusion of a war. Banquets to celebrate the coronation of William and Mary and the visits of the Princess of Denmark – the future Queen Anne – and the Earl of Stamford accounted for £44 1s. 11d. of Leicester corporation's outgoings of almost £532 in 1688–9.[27] Occasional alms to the sick, infirm and poor, the operation of a poor relief system and the disbursement of charitable funds may be grouped together in the accounts. In some towns the funds of those charities that were administered by the corporation were treated in separate sections, perhaps placed at the end of those relating to the corporation's own expenditure. The auditors' notes, perhaps querying some of the items, may be included after the expenditure section, concluding the annual account.

A characteristic feature of corporation accounts is that the payments sections are longer than those for revenues. This partly reflects the number and complexity of responsibilities which a corporation discharged and partly the fact that, in the pre-modern period at least, there was a tendency to note individual payments rather than gather related outgoings into single entries. Indeed, some of the entries in the typical account record small payments for very minor items, which may be difficult to interpret in terms of the information given and perhaps add little, in themselves, to an understanding of a corporation's expenditure. On the other hand, such detailed accounting does provide perhaps the only evidence for the recurrent and routine items which did not have to be brought before the council and its committees for approval. This applies to the payment of wages and salaries and the maintenance of buildings and equipment, for example, and so the period during which a post was held or an item of equipment remained operational can be discerned from the relevant payments. It should be possible to link those outgoings which were authorized by the council to the relevant entries in its minutes. The records of payments will normally show whether those decisions made by the council which required expenditure – and few did not – were implemented and, if they were, their cost and whether they were executed within the civic year in which the decisions were made or whether they required payments in subsequent years. Reference to the income side of the account may show that extraordinary revenue was raised to finance a particular project.

The accounts of the unreformed boroughs give the appearance of being well kept and in good order, but they should be treated with some circumspection, for they may conceal a more complex and uncertain state of affairs. Some boroughs got into considerable difficulties with their financial management. This was certainly the case at Leicester, where, by the mid 1830s, it seems that the chamberlains' accounts did not 'represent anything like a full picture of the Corporation's financial activity, its resources, or its indebtedness'.[28] One problem was that finances were commonly managed by part-time officers, who were fairly junior members of the council. The system of annual appointments allowed those who served as treasurer little opportunity to accumulate any degree of expertise, and the unpopularity of the post, with its demands on the time and even the pockets of the holders, meant that few would wish to serve in it for longer than was absolutely necessary. The demands were not great in all of the boroughs, for the budgets of many of them were not large enough to present their treasurers with any great difficulties. The average turnover of 178 boroughs investigated by the Municipal Corporations Commission in the 1830s was only roughly £5,400 and the smaller ones continued to operate with modest budgets throughout the nineteenth century.[29] The accounts of the borough corporation of St Ives, Huntingdonshire, incorporated in 1874, balanced at roughly £2,000 at the end of the century.[30] This is somewhat misleading, however, for the administrations in the larger towns did deal with far larger sums. The turnover of Newcastle-upon-Tyne's corporation was just over £40,000 in 1832–3, when its debt was almost £56,000, and Manchester's expenditure in 1838, the year in which it was incorporated, was £30,000.[31] Another reason for treating such accounts with caution is that they did not have to be open to public inspection and the audit was an internal one. Some boroughs did allow public perusal of their annual accounts and by the early nineteenth century a few published them, but this was not a general practice. The Municipal Corporations Act made it a requirement that the boroughs publish their accounts annually. This brought clarity and, hopefully, veracity to their presentation. It also considerably improved the chances of survival of the formal accounts, although not necessarily of the original bills and receipts.

Civic accounts changed in form and appearance in the nineteenth and early twentieth centuries, reflecting the expansion of civic finance, improved accounting techniques and the appointment of specialist staff to manage financial matters. Coventry corporation appointed a bailiff and a book-keeper in 1848, who were to look after its accounts, and other boroughs made similar appointments.[32] Greater responsibilities for housing, education, policing, the various aspects of welfare services and the provision of public utilities, with the increased staff costs in wages, salaries and pensions raised expenditure and revenues, which were drawn from a wider range of sources than hitherto. Such accounts also came to include forward budgeting in the form of annual, and perhaps also quarterly, estimates; a practice which was generally adopted from the mid nineteenth century onwards. The greater formality in the accounts does lead to some loss of detail, for it became common for the minor items of expenditure to be subsumed within larger categories, removing the element of informality characteristic of early modern accounts. They nevertheless remain invaluable for the evidence which they provide for the implementation of corporation policy and the conduct of routine administration.

## The records of the civic courts

The courts held by the incorporated boroughs had a range of jurisdictions over civil and minor criminal matters and also an important administrative function. Typically, the boroughs held their own quarter sessions, independent of those for the county, more frequent petty sessions and a court of record for small actions and claims, a court leet and view of frankpledge, a coroner's court and perhaps a separate piepowder court for the regulation of the markets and fairs. Their courts are specified in their charters of incorporation. That awarded to Boston in 1545 granted its corporation the power to make by-laws, the court leet, a court of record and a piepowder court, with the mayor as clerk of the market. It designated the mayor, recorder and senior aldermen as justices of the peace. Some boroughs were granted jurisdiction over other aspects of their affairs. Newcastle-upon-Tyne was exempt from Admiralty jurisdiction and held its own Conservancy Court, and Liverpool's Court of Passage was created to deal with cases arising from imports and exports passing through its port. The roles of the various civic courts as specified in the charters indicate a demarcation that was not always maintained as the courts' functions subsequently changed. Some courts fell into abeyance, such as those held by the staple towns, which were in decline by the sixteenth century and generally became moribund some time during the early-modern period, as did the remaining hundred courts. The structure of the courts within each borough, and their changing functions, should emerge from the records. These contain a range of matters and are in a variety of forms: rolls, volumes of minutes, orders and other transactions, and also files of indictments, pleas, recognizances, bonds, writs, narrations and depositions.

The views of frankpledge and courts leet had a manorial origin in the meetings of inhabitants. This is reflected in the lists of those who should appear at the court, which were still being compiled for some towns into the nineteenth century. During the early-modern period the chief, residual, purpose of such lists seems to have been to provide the names of those from whom the juries could be empanelled. They have a potential value for the demographic evidence which they contain, similar to the sources discussed in Chapter Four, but they may provide only a partial record of adult male residents, they may not have been kept up-to-date, and it may not be possible to determine the definition of what constituted adulthood in a particular town, or even if such a definition remained unchanged. The age of majority was not constant and was not the only criterion used. It seems that at Shrewsbury, and perhaps elsewhere, it was independent male householders who were listed, scarcely any of whom could have been teenagers, and such a definition means that those lists contain an economic and social bias, too.[33] Sessions papers also have oath rolls listing those who came to the court and were sworn.

A considerable part of the business transacted at the courts leet and quarter sessions was based upon the presentments and informations that were submitted to the court. The entries of the presentments are followed by orders to amend the fault within a specified time and the 'pain', or fine, which was to be levied upon failure to do so. They include a large proportion of environmental nuisances and breaches of the by-laws designed to protect public health and reduce fire risks. The nuisances presented in 1637 to the university's court leet at Oxford, which had jurisdiction throughout the city, included a number of citizens who had failed to maintain the pitching in the streets in front of their houses or to keep gutters and drains clear, had dangerously large stocks of furze for fuel upon their premises or had allowed piles of dung and garbage to accumulate. Some were presented for thatched buildings and others for melting tallow, which caused rather unpleasant pollution. The keeping of pigs was reported and attention was drawn to a brewer whose premises included an alley of tenants 'who live very nastily . . . enough to bring infections to the neighbours'. Tradesmen were presented for using unauthorized weights and measures. The presentments also included the parishes – chiefly for their failure to maintain streets, bridges and watercourses – and a number of the colleges, including Pembroke for not pitching the area around the college and not clearing away garbage, and Jesus for obstructing the highway with piles of timber. The city council was alluded to, but not named, in a presentment that pointed out that the conduit in the city centre was so placed as to cause an obstruction that was potentially dangerous on busy market days.[34] Similarly, the city chamberlains in Hereford had been presented at the court leet there a few years earlier because the High Cross in the market place needed repair and the common washing place was 'in decay'. Others who were presented at the courts leet in early-modern towns included those who kept unlicensed alehouses and brothels, drunkards, scolds, traders who were not freemen, catholic recusants and householders who had failed to contribute their share to a rate. Such presentments contain evidence of an economic, as well as a social and environmental, nature. For instance, eight of the nine men who were presented as 'strangers' in Winchester's town court in February 1685 were building workers; it was a time of considerable building activity in the city and two years earlier Charles II had set in motion the construction of a royal palace there.[35] The presentment of shipwrights at the Easter sessions in Newcastle-upon-Tyne in 1705, for refusing to work for their 'ancient wages', is evidence of a strike which was aimed at preserving existing wage levels.[36]

Wage problems came to the attention of the civic courts in other ways. For example, if such disputes spilled over into violence, then those who were apprehended were indicted at the sessions. In 1784 a number of tailors in Bath attempted to maintain their wage levels by intimidating those who were prepared to work for lower rates, breaking the windows of one man and beating him up and threatening another with a pistol, for which three men appeared before the sessions.[37] This kind of crime was not untypical of the felonies and misdemeanours that were dealt with by the civic magistrates. In the second half of the seventeenth century the Portsmouth sessions handled cases of theft, housebreaking, receipt of stolen goods, arson, rape, fornication, bastardy, bigamy, adultery, illicit gaming and bribery. The abuse of authority, royal and civic, often in quite colourful terms, led to a number of appearances before the justices and action was also taken against those guilty of sabbath breaking and profanation of holy days, while the laws against catholic recusants and meetings of protestant dissenters were intermittently enforced. The economic measures against irregular trading, forestallers of the market, regraters and engrossers were implemented and disputes over apprenticeships were also dealt with by the Portsmouth magistrates.[38] The records of such courts include the indictments, writs of summons, examinations and depositions of witnesses, the recognizances for the appearances of the accused and the convictions, with a note of the penalty or sentence imposed. It may be possible to detect some pattern to the petty crimes committed, which may be related to changed economic and social conditions within a town. As the trades and statuses of the accused, their sureties and those making depositions are usually entered, a relationship between some kinds of offences and trades or statuses may emerge. The age and address of a deponent was also given, together with some indication of how long he or she had lived in a place or known the accused, which provides useful evidence for migration, residence patterns and the area from which people came to a town to trade. The contents of the depositions are a source of evidence, yet it is often of an incidental nature, lacking in context, and is useful only if it can be linked to circumstances which have been established from other material.

The presentation and punishment of breaches of the law was one part of the justices' operations and it merged into the other side of their activities, which were administrative, in the promulgation of by-laws and orders. In this respect they acted as an extension of the common council's administration. Much of their attention was focused upon the licensing of inns and alehouses and the collection of rates. In addition to such routine matters, they also acted to make arrangements for providing assistance to individuals or sections of the community stricken by plague, flood, fire or other misfortunes. They were able to respond to emergencies more swiftly than was the council. The Gloucester justices gave orders for help to be provided for the inhabitants of two of the riverside parishes of the city, which were so badly flooded when the Severn overflowed during the particularly wet summer of 1640 that boats had to be used to get to some of the houses.[39] Some of the orders issued at the sessions were responses to presentments recommending a course of action or series of measures. Thus, in the summer of 1665, when the jury at Hereford outlined steps which should be taken to minimize the risk of plague spreading from London, these were immediately issued by the magistrates as a set of orders. Similarly, the grand jury's presentment to the sessions at Bristol after a fire in the city in 1670 criticized the response to the emergency and the unsatisfactory condition of the fire-fighting equipment and requested that appropriate orders should be made to correct the deficiencies. Proclamations were also made against specific nuisances, such as the cattle and swine roaming the streets of Norwich and the throwing of fireworks, which was banned in Restoration Exeter. In 1677 an order was made in Hereford against speeding within the built-up area when a fine was instituted for those riding a horse through the streets at a gallop, although an exception was made if the horse was being offered for sale when, it was recognized, its capabilities had to be demonstrated.[40] The justices also had a role to play in economic regulation, setting maximum prices for certain basic items of food and drink and also the wage levels of some groups of workers. An order of the Worcester justices of 1648 fixed the weekly and daily rates of pay for the journeymen workers in the cloth industry there, and also their hours of work, which were from five o'clock in the morning until eight o'clock in the evening.[41] Other by-laws and orders issued by the justices typically dealt with matters arising from apprenticeship arrangements, the settlement of paupers, water supply and the lighting, watching and cleansing of the streets. It was a common practice for a codification of the by-laws to be entered from time to time and perhaps also printed.

The county quarter sessions handled a similar range of business to the borough sessions and their jurisdictions included the unincorporated and small towns which were not entitled to hold their own sessions. Their records should also be checked for material relating to the inhabitants of the incorporated boroughs who were indicted at the county sessions, or who petitioned them regarding matters which fell within their purview, rather than that of the borough magistrates. The county quarter sessions papers form major collections in the county record offices.

Control of the markets was an important function of civic administration and in many boroughs was entrusted to a court which was kept distinct from the other borough courts. The origin of the market courts lay in the medieval courts of piepowder, *curia pedis pulverizati*; literally, the 'Court of the Dusty Feet', or the 'Court of the Pedlars'. Their authority was restricted to the area of the market on market days and also on the days on which fairs were held. Such courts were generally held before the mayor and the aldermen or bailiffs, as stewards of the market. The records of the piepowder courts contain regulations governing the operation of the market, concerning such matters as the weights and measures used, the hours of trading, the licensing of non-freemen who rented stalls and the rates charged by the carriers who served the market. The regulations at Ipswich included elaborate rules respecting the sale of such commodities as hides, tallow and cloth.[42] Presentments of breaches of the regulations and the measures taken to enforce them – such as the fines levied upon traders who were overcharging – should be entered in the records, together with notes of cases of trespass or minor criminal offences committed within the court's jurisdiction. These courts also recorded debts contracted within the market, typically noting the parties, their addresses and the sums involved, but rarely giving the nature or cause of the debt. Nevertheless, such information can be used to provide an indication of the typical scale of the debts and the area from which people came to attend the market. The books which record the sales at the periodic livestock fairs, for the purpose of levying the tolls due on the sales, contain similar evidence, but also give the numbers and type of animals sold and their price. Fairs generally drew buyers and sellers from a wider area than did markets; slightly over a half of the purchasers of horses at the Shrewsbury fair in 1608 came from outside Shropshire.[43] The survival of such toll books has not been especially good, however. Moreover, it seems likely that many of the transactions were not entered, so that the toll could be evaded, although horse fairs were more closely regulated than those for sheep and cattle.

The civic courts of record, known by a variety of designations, dealt with civil actions that had arisen within their jurisdictions. Some towns actually obtained powers to prevent their freemen from suing in other courts in actions which could be handled within the borough court. It was not unusual for there to be a limit to the scale of the actions which such a court could handle, however. Leominster's charter of 1554 limited pleas of debts in its courts to £5, that granted to Tewkesbury 21 years later stipulated an upper limit of £2 and High Wycombe's charter of 1558 allowed it to deal with cases up to £20.[44] In contrast, the mayor's court at Oxford was empowered to deal with all personal actions which had arisen within its jurisdiction, regardless of the scale of the debt.[45] From the late seventeenth century a number of towns obtained Acts of Parliament to establish 'courts of conscience', sometimes known as courts of requests, for dealing with small debt cases, which may reflect increasing commercial activity during the period. Gloucester and Hull set up such courts by Acts of 1689 and 1761 respectively, with upper limits of £2 on the actions brought before them, although this was raised to £5 at Hull in 1808.[46]

The courts of record met relatively frequently and much of their business was concerned with small debts and a range of minor actions, including those relating to property, such as trespass, and retention of goods. The information entered in their records was not very full, perhaps only the names of the parties and the nature and value of enrolments of bonds entered into under statute merchant agreements – the more informative of which give an indication of the nature of the debt incurred – as well as enrolled deeds and wills. The petty court at Ipswich served as a court of orphans and so copies of relevant wills are entered amongst its proceedings. Such orphans' courts were separate entities in a number of cities, established to act as guardians of the estates of the orphaned children of freemen. The enrolled wills of those whose estates were taken into the care of the courts provide useful evidence for the scale of their possessions and for family relationships, but they are a biased sample, for non-freemen were excluded and it seems that orphans whose goods were of low value were not dealt with by such courts. Nor are the numbers of such wills particularly large. A court of orphans was granted to Worcester corporation by the terms of its charter of 1555, but only 127 wills were enrolled in its register in the following 53 years.[47] The money which came to the courts from the orphans' estates was lent out to citizens, who entered into bonds to repay it, and their identity can be established from their recognizances, which should also be enrolled in the courts' records. In some cities, such as Exeter, the court provided cheap loans for the corporation itself, effectively subsidising the civic finances.

It was common for boroughs to hold the right to appoint coroners, to operate within their jurisdictions. In some towns the choice of coroner was left to the mayor and burgesses, or a specified group of senior councillors. This was the case at Gloucester and, by the terms of its 1483 charter, the mayor took his oath of office before the coroner. In other boroughs, such as Lancaster, the mayor served as coroner during his term of office and so there was no need to choose a separate coroner.[48] The duties of the coroners included some criminal jurisdictions, but their records are chiefly of interest for the inquests held into unexplained deaths and those which occurred in prison. Apart from their evidence on the numbers and causes of accidental deaths and the incidence of murders, the inquests may show that there were some social patterns to the deaths investigated. By far the majority of the suicides recorded in eighteenth-century Bath were committed by servants and labourers, for example.[49] By this period the coroners' records can be used in conjunction with reports in newspapers, which tended to carry accounts of the cases investigated, sometimes expressed in rather lurid terms.

The eighteenth and nineteenth centuries saw changes in the effective operation of the civic courts, many of which declined as they were superseded by others. This was the case with the view of frankpledge and court leet, whose activities gradually merged with those of the sessions of the peace in many boroughs. Gloucester's view of frankpledge was apparently still thriving in the early eighteenth century, but was meeting only once a year by the 1780s and continued to decline thereafter. Other courts also came to deal with a contracting range of business. The mayor's court at Exeter nominally shared jurisdiction with the provost's court over all real and personal actions orginating in the city, but during the eighteenth century it came to be chiefly concerned with matters relating to the freedom.[50] The appointment of improvement commissions tended to draw responsibility for health and environmental matters away from the courts. In many boroughs the regular court business came to be concentrated at the petty and quarter sessions and court of record. The reforms of the nineteenth century removed many jurisdictional anomalies and abolished courts which had become wholly or largely moribund. There were a few exceptions nevertheless, notably the Tolsey Court at Bristol, which was an example of the survival of a piepowder court, and Liverpool's Court of Passage, both of which were extinguished by the Courts Act of 1971.

The manorial courts remained intact in those towns which continued to be administered through the manorial apparatus until they were incorporated in the nineteenth century. This was the case at Manchester and the functions and expanding business of its court can be traced in the records, which have survived and are in print in 12 volumes, edited by J.P. Earwaker as *The Court Leet Records of the Manor of Manchester* (1884–90). They illustrate its role as the local governing authority, promulgating by-laws, suppressing nuisances, levying rates and appointing officers, who numbered over 100 by the late seventeenth century. The survival of the records of the courts which administered the small unincorporated boroughs has not been so good, presumably because many ceased to exist during the sixteenth and seventeenth centuries and they had no immediate successor bodies. Witney's borough court became defunct during the mid seventeenth century and had certainly ceased operating by the 1670s. Two of its court books have survived, covering the period 1538–1610, but the related papers to which they refer have been lost.[51]

Such courts handled little criminal business, but they were used by suitors seeking the recovery of small debts and they also had administrative functions over matters relating to economic regulation, poor law, health, apprenticeship and property.

The preservation rate for the records of the courts of the incorporated boroughs should have been much better than it was for those of the unincorporated ones which fell into abeyance, but even so it has not been especially good, certainly not as good as that for the council minutes and accounts, in most cases. The only remaining complete record for the view of frankpledge and sessions of the peace for sixteenth-century Worcester is that for 1553, for example, and the records of the Portmanmoot at Leicester – the borough's court of record – were despatched to the destructor at the end of the nineteenth century.[52] Other towns may have fared better in this respect, but complete sets of records for all of the various courts seem to be comparatively rare. Yet, while the main series may be incomplete, most corporation archives have some miscellaneous legal papers, perhaps including communications from the assize judges and papers relating to cases which involved the corporation, directly or indirectly, that were heard in the courts at Westminster.

# Chapter Seven
# GOVERNMENT, PARLIAMENT AND THE COURTS

The papers of government and Parliament are in some ways the most daunting for local historians, chiefly because of their bulk and the complexity of the administrative, judicial and legislative processes which produced them. There are three principal guides to the collections, providing signposts through the maze. The *Guide to the Contents of the Public Record Office* is in three volumes (1963–8) and there is a further explanation of the public records, with local historians' needs particularly in mind, in Philip Riden's *Record Sources for Local History* (1987). The manuscript parliamentary material is described in Maurice F. Bond, *Guide to the Records of Parliament* (1971).

## Privy Council records and the state papers

The intermittent contact between urban authorities and central government in the early-modern period was concerned with many matters, ranging from the levying of taxation to anxiety about the production and circulation of potentially seditious literature. Much of it is recorded in the Privy Council's registers and in the classes of documents known collectively as the domestic state papers, which have been aptly described as a 'voluminous conglomeration'.[1] The contents of these records are made relatively accessible through a number of series of printed calendars. Those of the Privy Council are calendared in S.H. Nicholas's *Privy Council of England, Proceedings and Ordinances . . .*, from 1386 to 1542, and in the volumes of the *Acts of the Privy Council of England* which cover the Council's registers for the period 1542–1631. The registers themselves are in the Chancery Lane section of the Public Record Office, class PC 2; those for 1637–45 have been issued in facsimile form. Its papers constitute class PC 1, but this contains no material from before 1698. Worse still, there are only two late-sixteenth-century volumes of the proceedings of the Council's subordinate Council in the Marches of Wales, which sat until 1688, and none for its other regional subsidiary, the Council in the North, which was not revived after the Interregnum. The volumes of the *Letters and Papers, Foreign and Domestic, of the Reign of Henry VIII* incorporate material from the state papers and collections outside the public records, while the *Calendars of State Papers, Domestic*, which continue to 1704, deal only with the state papers themselves. A calendar

112

produced by the List and Index Society covers the state papers of George I's reign and there is also a *Calendar of Home Office Papers of the Reign of George III, 1760–1775.* The Privy Council served as the focus of government for much of the early-modern period, but its importance was somewhat diminished during the tenure of William and Robert Cecil as Secretaries of State, until the latter's death in 1612, and the balance shifted to the secretariat more decisively and more permanently during the late seventeenth century. In 1689 the secretariat was divided into the southern and northern departments which, in 1782, became the Home Office and Foreign Office respectively. Many of the Privy Council's papers were lodged amongst the state papers, as were those of the Secretaries of State, although there was no State Paper Office as such until the early seventeenth century. It follows that both the PC and SP classes in the public records should be searched for evidence of the government's concern with and involvement in civic affairs.

The Privy Council dealt with matters at all levels: the large-scale issues of national policies, the general concerns of urban government, particular problems in specific towns and cases of personal grievance. It handled the granting of charters to boroughs and guild companies, a function which it retained after it had lost many of its other roles. Indeed, by the 1835 Municipal Corporations Act, it had to approve the division of boroughs into wards and the number of councillors for each ward, and it also had the power to disallow by-laws made by borough corporations. Because of this aspect of its role, the Privy Council acted to resolve jurisdictional disputes. There was no shortage of these in the early-modern town. They arose between corporations and guild companies, the county justices and the ecclesiastical authorities. Disputes between different companies were also referred to the Council, for each was jealous of its rights and privileges and anxious that they should not be encroached upon, and of course this also applied to the borough authorities themselves. The Council also took an interest in the political composition of corporations and the holders of their offices. It intervened at Carlisle when, in 1567, a mayor was elected whom it regarded as unsatisfactory; ten years later it summoned before it the two rival mayors of Dover, one of whom had been chosen in defiance of its recommendation. It received and acted upon appeals from individual officers and councillors. In 1619 it ordered the reinstatement of John Finch, the recorder of Canterbury, and of Philip Treherne, a member of Hereford's common council who had been dismissed and imprisoned, allegedly for his vociferous objection to the way in which the funds for obtaining a new charter had been raised.[2]

Another of the government's major concerns was the maintenance of law and order. It investigated the causes of disturbances, attempted to mitigate the effects of food shortages, high prices, economic recession and unemployment, and in so doing gathered considerable evidence on such matters. The pattern of popular unrest in early Stuart London can be determined from the Privy Council's records, for example. The disturbances there which came to its attention ranged from fairly minor affairs – some of which were little more than insults and abuse offered to foreign diplomats and their retinues – to riots, such as the one in 1617 when a numerous mob wrecked and then began to demolish a playhouse in Drury Lane.[3] Some disorderly incidents had religious overtones, as predominantly puritan civic governments attempted to suppress festivals and revelries in defiance of popular opinion and the policy of the church's hierarchy. Food shortages and high prices were likely to cause unrest and the Council took an increased interest in the grain trade in times of dearth, attempting to control it by means of detailed orders. It also sought to limit the quantities of grain which went to the brewers and its anxieties over the numbers of alehouses also increased when harvests were bad. Other users of grain were warned against unnecessarily high consumption, or even banned from operating for a time. Thus, in 1630 the Council sent an order to Norwich prohibiting the making of starch there.[4] Unemployment, leading to poverty, when coupled with high food prices, was also a potential cause of disorder. It was partly for that reason, and also because of its wider importance, that the cloth industry was a cause of concern, especially during the recession which it experienced in the early seventeenth century. The industry's difficulties focused the council's attention more closely upon it, and particularly upon the West Country clothing towns. This produced enquiries from the Council regarding the scale and organization of the industry and its arrangements for the supply of wool. In 1616, for example, it sent out an enquiry requesting intelligence regarding the numbers of looms in operation, the numbers of workmen employed and the changes in prosperity which had been experienced over the previous few years.[5] Such investigations and the petitions directed to the Council from the clothing towns help to build up a picture of the industry's organization and changing fortunes. Attention was drawn to the extent of urban poverty, and the problems which it caused, during economic recessions and periods of high prices, when the Council's intermittent promptings and reminders relating to poor relief became more frequent. They culminated in its issue of the Book of Orders in 1631, which was a codification of the existing law and a signal to the local authorities that its terms should be observed.

Government concern with the environment was chiefly related to public health and the risk of epidemics in cities and towns, where the concentration of population made the problem a potentially serious one. Its actions in this respect were partly aimed at limiting the spread of an epidemic which had begun, and partly preventative. It recommended the detailed measures to be taken in the event of an outbreak, such as the quarantining of victims at home or in a pesthouse and the prohibition of unnecessary public gatherings. Thus, in 1630, it warned the mayor of Norwich that the corporation's midsummer feast might have to be cancelled because of the danger of plague.[6] The steps which it ordered were generally those standard ones which the civic magistrates would take in such circumstances, but the Privy Council used its position to co-ordinate information and give advanced, and official, warnings of the onset of disease. The Council also took steps to minimize the dangers of an outbreak. For example, it recognized that overcrowding put pressure upon the system of poor relief and created a health hazard, and so investigated cases of overpopulation which came to its attention. In 1584 it intervened at Cambridge, ordering a survey of the houses there which had been subdivided in the previous ten years, and an enumeration of their occupants.[7]

The Privy Council also issued instructions concerning other environmental matters. In 1619, for example, the Council made orders prohibiting thatching, stipulating the use of stone or brick for chimneys and regulating the storage of fuel at both Cambridge, in response to promptings by the university, and Stratford-upon-Avon, where the common council had petitioned that it was apprehensive of not having sufficient authority to make and effectively enforce the orders required.[8] The Council did indeed become involved with the minutiae of local administration, albeit irregularly. An example of this arose in the case of Philip Sherwood, whose alehouse was suppressed by the justices at Bath in 1621, but was restored in the following year on the Council's orders. This incident was part of a larger wrangle between the government and local justices over licensing arrangements.[9] All matters involving the government and the civic authorities have to be assessed in their wider context, and both local and governmental records consulted in order to establish as complete a view of the evidence as possible.

The assize judges on circuit were an integral part of the executive's operations in the early-modern period, especially during the reigns of Elizabeth and the early Stuarts. This involved them in an assessment of the effectiveness of the magistrates – correcting and prompting them when necessary – ensuring that the Council's policies were carried out, that legislation was complied with and also that the Council was kept informed of economic, religious and political conditions in the provinces. The matters which they dealt with were broadly those outlined above. They acted to enforce the observance of the Book of Orders, for example, and to oversee the regulation of the grain trade and the licensing of alehouses.[10] In some cases they were instructed by the Council to investigate a specific occurrence which had come to its attention, such as the disputed mayoral election at Oxford in 1620. In other instances they acted directly in response to petitions and complaints addressed to them, as with the petition from the inhabitants of a parish close to Worcester which had been put to the expense of providing relief for the poor refugees from the city's suburbs during and after the Civil War. An example of economic conditions coming to their notice is to be found in the report of 1629 in which the Norfolk circuit judges warned the Privy Council of the fragile state of the cloth trade in Bury St Edmunds. This report is amongst the state papers, which, together with the Privy Council's registers, contain many of the assize judges' communications.[11] The ASSI classes themselves are in the Public Record Office, Chancery Lane. They include order books for the western circuit, 1629–85,[12] but few other documents which can be classified as 'administrative', although there are some entries of that nature in other classes within the ASSI group.

It is less easy to summarize the state papers. They contain the records of the secretariat, some of those of the Privy Council and the assize judges and a miscellany of other papers. All of the concerns discussed above are to be found amongst them in the form of orders, petitions, reports and correspondence. A few examples from the early months of 1692 are indicative of the kind of material which they contain for the late seventeenth century, but they should not be regarded as representative of the whole range of matters to be found in this archive. They show that new charters were requested by Plymouth and Plympton because of the uncertainties arising from the proceedings against their rights in the reigns of Charles II and James II. A warrant was issued to prepare a charter for incorporating the grocers, mercers and drapers of Tiverton, and a bill was to be prepared by which six aldermen of the City of London were to be added to the list of justices of the peace. An order was made for garrisoning and victualling Plymouth. Other military matters had arisen. Attention had been drawn to problems at Northampton, where the innholders, victuallers, corn chandlers and farriers had claimed £563 13s. 10d. unpaid for the quartering of five troops of horse, and Portsmouth, whose mayor was fearful of billeting 60 new recruits in the town in case he should be sued by the householders. A letter was sent to the mayor of Exeter regarding the master of a Danish vessel, a suspected smuggler who was in Exeter gaol, ordering him to send the prisoner to Whitehall for questioning. It was also ordered that the imminent presentation to the living of the Chard should be suspended, following the receipt of a petition to the crown from the inhabitants – the order was later rescinded – and a memorandum noted a case of bribery at an election at Chippenham. These are the bare outlines; the calendar has more information, and virtually all of the papers give much fuller information than do their entries in the calendars.[13]

With the evolution of the duties of the Privy Council and the Home Office in the eighteenth and nineteenth centuries, both bodies came to exercise oversight of a number of functions that were directly concerned with urban administration. In addition to the Council's responsibilities respecting borough constitutions, its committees dealt with health and education matters during the nineteenth century, while the Home Office undertook supervision over police and fire services, which were administered by the local authorities, and from 1829 held direct control of the police force in the metropolis. The expanding range of matters which came within the Home Office's jurisdiction can be traced in its papers in the Public Record Office at Kew. Amongst the most useful classes are HO 42 and HO 44, containing the incoming papers for 1782–1861, with a divide between the classes at 1820; HO 43 for outgoing correspondence 1782–1898; and HO 52, which has 'municipal and provincial' correspondence for 1820–50. In addition, HO 45 consists of material known as 'registered papers' and is accessible for the periods 1841–79 and after 1924 through the Public Record Office's lists, and for 1879–1924 through a series of List and Index Society volumes. A search in this archive can be narrowed down, both topically and chronologically, by first identifying contact between the Home Office and a particular town from the latter's own records.

## The records of Parliament

As with the records of the Privy Council and secretariat, those of Parliament are relatively accessible through printed calendars and proceedings. The proceedings of the two Houses are summarized in their *Journals*; those of the Lords date from 1509 and those of the Commons from 1547. The main papers of the House of Lords are calendared in a sequence of the Historical Manuscripts Commission's published reports, running from its *Third Report* to appendix VI of its *Fourteenth Report*. These reports cover the period to 1693. A similar, although separately issued, series of *House of Lords Papers* continues the calendar to 1718. The papers are in the House of Lords record office. As well as the official records of the House, the collection also contains material of a different nature, including private papers, such as the letters written by Robert Gray, a London merchant, to his wife between 1606 and 1618 as he visited fairs around the country to buy wares.[14]

Much of the contact between the urban corporations, groups such as the guild companies and individual citizens on the one hand, and the two Houses of Parliament on the other, was initiated in petitions. From the late sixteenth century onwards, petitioning was an accepted way of submitting requests, protests and information to both Houses. It became the required practice to submit a petition before a Private Bill could be introduced and petitions were also submitted if a hearing in the House of Lords was to be requested regarding a supposed miscarriage of justice. Others were prepared seeking redress in the event of a wrong, requesting some action by Parliament or objecting to a measure which was pending or had been passed. Between the late eighteenth and early twentieth centuries Parliament received tens of thousands of 'public petitions' which sought political, economic or social reform, and these commonly contained many signatures.

Petitions drew attention to matters of many kinds, relating not only to civic administration and jurisdictional questions, but also to social problems, the state of local industries, the impact of overseas trade and the circumstances of individuals. Some described events which had occurred, a calamity perhaps, such as storm damage to a harbour or a flood, while others warned of the possible consequences of a particular course of action if it was not reversed. The excise duties imposed in the 1690s to help finance the wars of William III drew a stream of petitions from those working in the affected industries, for example. The glassmakers in and around Stourbridge in Worcestershire submitted seven petitions to the House of Commons between 1696 and 1699 aimed at the abolition of the new duty on glass wares and expressing, in the characteristically graphic terms of the period, the likely effects of its continuation, which were that 'the Petitioners and their Families must starve, or be maintained by their Parishes'. All of these petitions are noted in the House of Commons *Journals.*[15] The Commons also received many petitions concerned with contested elections to the House, especially during the eighteenth and early nineteenth centuries. Considerable evidence on a range of concerns is contained in the petitions which were submitted for the purpose of introducing, furthering, modifying and, indeed, opposing, Private Bills. These Bills were generally introduced into the House of Lords in the first instance. Petitions of this kind carried a great deal of information, for their presenters had to support their case by including relevant arguments and evidence, while those who were counter-petitioning were bound either to present new material or to offer an alternative interpretation of that which had already been submitted.

Only a few of the original petitions to the Commons have survived; they relate to the period 1621–49. The bulk of those from before 1834 were lost in the fire which gutted the Houses of Parliament in that year, and thereafter it was the practice to destroy petitions after the Select Committee appointed for the purpose had investigated and summarized them and chosen representative ones for printing. The receipt of petitions is, however, noted in the *Journals* after 1571 and in the House's Votes and Proceedings after 1680. For the period 1742–1833 the full texts of many petitions are given in the Votes and Proceedings or the many volumes of its supplements and appendices. The presentation of a petition to the House of Lords is recorded in its *Journals*. For the late seventeenth and eighteenth centuries in particular, its *Journals* include the texts of some petitions and extensive extracts from or summaries of others, but these represent only a small part of the total number received by that House. The preservation of the originals has been erratic and few presented before 1621 are extant. Those which have survived, of which there are 3,200, are generally to be found in the main papers of the House. The nature of the other evidence which exists varies according to the type of Bill, whether it was opposed and its date. It includes deposited plans and statements (pp. 28–9), judges' reports, from 1706, which give some guidance on the validity of conflicting claims, evidence taken by committees – which are in files among the main papers and, from 1835, in Books of Evidence – and departmental reports.

The progress of Bills can be traced using the *Journals* of the two Houses. For the nineteenth and twentieth centuries further detail is available from *Hansard's Parliamentary Debates* and, for the period 1828–41, the *Mirror of Parliament*. Both of these sources summarize the debates; the speeches were recorded in *Hansard's* only after it was designated as the official record of Parliament in 1909. There are also the 70 volumes of Ross's *Parliamentary Record*, covering the years 1861–1939, in which 'Votes and Proceedings in Public Matters' are summarized. Those Bills which passed both Houses and received the Royal Assent are recorded in the *Statutes at Large* until 1870 and thereafter in *The Public General Statutes*. The period of the Civil War and Interregnum is covered in *Acts and Ordinances of the Interregnum*, edited by C.H. Firth and R.S. Rait. Not all Bills were printed and those which exist only in manuscript form are in the House of Lords record office. There is also a valuable *Index to Local and Personal Acts, 1801 to 1947*, which indicates the nature of each Act, its reference and, where applicable, the measure by which it was repealed. Indices of the relevant Acts have also been compiled for individual cities and towns, such as Lawence Gomme and Seagar Berry's *London Statutes . . . From 1750 to 1907*.

## Parliamentary Papers

A very considerable body of evidence collected by the government is contained in the Parliamentary Papers, commonly called the 'Blue Books'. They include, in the Accounts and Papers, the reports of officers and inspectors, information assembled by the government's departments and agencies, and other material requested by or presented to Parliament and published on its orders. In the early and mid nineteenth century both Houses made numerous Orders and Addresses for papers concerning information and statistics. These were later established as Command Papers or Act Papers. Many of the data in the Parliamentary Papers are of a statistical nature, on trade, employment and demography, for example. Bills introduced into Parliament are included and they also contain the reports of the committees of the Houses of Parliament, and Royal Commissions. These investigations were linked to a considerable extent to the reforming legislation passed during the nineteenth century, for the procedure was to obtain information on a subject under review, prior to drafting a Bill, or taking other action. Elections, health, sanitation, housing, poor law matters, transport, education, prisons, asylums, vagrancy, trade, industry and working conditions were amongst the subjects that were investigated. The administrations of the boroughs were scrutinized – most notably by the Royal Commission of the 1830s – especially if there was a suggestion of corruption or electoral malpractice, as there was in Barnstaple in the early 1850s, which led to investigations by Commission and Select Committee. Religion also attracted attention from time to time, as in the 1850s, when a Select Committee of the House of Lords reported on the 'Deficiency of Means of Spiritual Instruction and Places of Divine Worship in the Metropolis and in other Populous Districts'.[16] As Parliamentary concern with, and involvement in, such matters increased, so the evidence which it collected grew in scale. The subjects examined reflected the major current concerns. In the 1840s, in the aftermath of the outbreaks of cholera, the health and sanitation of towns attracted attention, and in the 1880s various aspects of their housing problems came under scrutiny. Some enquiries were directed specifically to particular towns, or to urban areas, but others were more general. In an increasingly urbanized country, many which were not explicitly instructed to investigate the cities and towns were, in practice, concerned to a great extent with urban conditions.

The reports of the inspectors, Parliamentary Committees and Royal Commissions consist of their findings and recommendations, with the transcripts of the sessions in which selected witnesses gave evidence and were questioned. The contents of a report were coloured by the nature and purpose of the enquiry, that is, whether it was designed to deal with a specific and restricted matter or was of a more general nature, for those carrying out the investigation were circumscribed by their terms of reference. The way in which they conducted their enquiry also affected the nature of the evidence which it generated, for they may not have allowed their witnesses to expand their replies or to digress, and the slant which one or more of the investigators gave to the questions may have produced a bias in the answers. The representativeness and usefulness of the contents of the enquiries' reports were also coloured by the choice of witnesses, their expertise and the frankness of their contributions. Some witnesses made written submissions of evidence in addition to their verbal testimonies. These were characteristically of material which was not easily summarized, such as statistical returns. In addition, some relevant facts and figures were already available to those who were conducting an enquiry, were mentioned by them to the witnesses in the course of the questioning and so appear in the records of the investigations. Other written evidence was sent by the officers of organizations who had been invited to reply to questions forwarded to them by the investigators. Those sent to the borough corporations were generally answered by the town clerk, for example. The range of issues examined and the breadth of the evidence submitted make the reports valuable sources, especially on social and economic matters. Indeed, they were drawn upon by contemporary novelists seeking authentic background information.

Some indication of the scale and range of the evidence submitted to such enquiries is provided by two examples. One is the second Report of the Committee on Town Holdings of 1888, which investigated tenurial arrangements, with a view to establishing, if possible, the desirability of increasing property ownership amongst the working classes. The 42 witnesses who gave evidence included the town clerks of Wolverhampton and Southport, land agents from Birmingham and Sheffield, the manager of a building society in Leeds, the surveyor of Lord Portman's London estate, a builder in Nottingham, a solicitor in Devonport, Bury corporation's chairman of finance, an architect and surveyor from Bristol and a grocer and a boot maker in Great Malvern. The evidence was set out in 15,047 paragraphs, which covered 660 pages, with ten appendices. The second is the Royal Commission on the Depression of Trade and Industry, which reported in 1886, having assembled evidence from an equally wide range of sources, including one set of questionnaires that was sent out to local chambers of commerce and another which was directed to workers' associations. The answers, printed in the Commission's *Reports*, were received from the chambers of commerce in 40 towns in England and Wales, listing the chief local trades and industries, assessing the fluctuations in trade over the previous 20 years and the depth of the current recession and giving their opinions on the causes of the changes. Many of the replies blamed overseas competition, but some also pointed to other factors. The chambers of commerce for Dudley and Wolverhampton both took the opportunity to point the finger at the 'unfair, unequal, and excessive railway rates' levied on their products and to deplore the monopoly of transport which the railway companies had enjoyed since they had taken over control of the local canals. The questions addressed to the workers' associations were similarly designed to gain an indication of the effects of the recession, but they also asked for information on the numbers working in a trade, the numbers in the association, the rates of pay, whether wages were assessed by piece work or time work, and the apprenticeship or other training arrangements in the trade. Many of the replies were brief and not all of the questions were answered in every case, but these returns nevertheless contain a great deal of information on the organization and operation of industry.[17]

The amount of material in this category presents problems. Furthermore, the titles of some of the papers are no certain guide to their contents. The report entitled *Statements of Men Living in Certain Selected Districts of London*, issued in 1887, is a case in point. Official indices to the papers were produced periodically and the individual *Reports* are generally indexed. Some of the eighteenth-century *Reports* are contained in the *Journals* of the Houses of Parliament, which have their own indices, or in the 16 volumes of *Reports (1715– 1802) from Committees of the House of Commons printed by order of the House and not inserted in the Journals* (1803–20).

Hansard's *Catalogue and Breviate of Parliamentary Papers, 1696–1834* (1953) and P. and G. Ford's *Select List of British Parliamentary Papers, 1833–1899* (1953) provide finding aids for the eighteenth- and nineteenth-century papers, arranged by subjects. P. and G. Ford also published three volumes of their *Breviate of Parliamentary Papers* covering the period 1900–54 (1951, 1957, 1961). In addition, an annual list of the Stationery Office's publications has appeared since 1837. A comprehensive subject index of the Parliamentary Papers is in progress, beginning with a *Subject Catalogue of the House of Commons Parliamentary Papers 1801–1900*, edited by Peter Cockburn (1988–).

## The courts

Of the various central courts operating in the sixteenth and early seventeenth centuries, Star Chamber was most closely identified as an instrument of government control, although much of the business which it dealt with was unconnected with this aspect of its role. The court of Star Chamber was produced by the separation of the executive and judicial functions of the Council during the reign of Henry VIII. The process was completed in 1540 when the court was given its own clerk and minute book; its identity was then clearly distinct from that of the Council. The cases which fell within its jurisdiction included those involving riot, a term which was interpreted fairly widely, and assaults upon those in authority. Examples from York in the reign of Henry VIII mention a number of instances of manslaughter in affrays, including a street fight between the retainers of rival gentry, and the case of Richard Heden, a lawyer, who was set upon in his inn by several assailants, who drove him into a corner with their blows and 'broke sonder boyth hys sworde and bokeler' so that he was 'lykly to have beyn slayn' and was only saved because the neighbours heard the commotion.[18] The court also dealt with jurisdictional disputes involving corporations, and suits between them. The dissension between the sheriff and the mayor of Bristol relating to the payment by the sheriff of the fee farm rents due to the crown in 1518 came before the Star Chamber, and the evidence presented includes much detail on the corporation's financial arrangements and the sums involved, as well as a reference to the city's 'great desolacion', with about 800 households 'desolate vacante and decayed'. Factional conflicts within the corporation of Gloucester in the early seventeenth century were so bitter and involved that they led to a series of cases in the court.[19] The chief interest of the evidence generated by some cases is incidental to the actual cause at issue. For instance, in a wrangle between the vicar of Hull and the corporation regarding the fencing of the churchyard, heard in 1608, both parties agreed that there were then separatists in the town.[20]

Another function of the Star Chamber court was to enforce royal proclamations. The proclamations for 1485–1646 are reproduced in five volumes edited by Paul Hughes and James Larkin (1964–83).[21] The procedure of the court was that either the Attorney General or a plaintiff initiated a case. Two examples from the reign of James I illustrate this in actions concerning buildings erected within two miles of the City of London, contrary to a number of proclamations. In the first, the trustees administering a charitable property in High Holborn brought a case against a group of 'greedy & covitously minded persons' for building houses in Holborn and Bloomsbury. The second one was begun by the Attorney General against two men who had put up houses in Drury Lane and the Strand, one of them on a site where a house had previously been pulled down on the Privy Council's orders. Both cases provide considerable detail and record the defendants' responses to the charges.[22] They are fairly typical of the court's papers, which consist chiefly of bills, answers and depositions. There are no surviving decrees and orders. The bulk of the material is from the reigns of Elizabeth I and James I, and the court was abolished in 1641.

The court of Star Chamber's function was comparatively distinct and limited and it had a relatively short life. This was not the case with all of the central courts, for by the early-modern period the long-established ones had developed a number of judicial functions. King's Bench had both criminal and civil jurisdiction, on its crown and plea sides respectively. The files of indictments on the crown side can be used to establish the incidence and nature of crimes and of deaths that resulted from violence. They are not a self-contained category of records, however, for some of the papers which should have been kept in the Ancient Indictments of that court are in the assize records. The criminal records of the assize courts consist of similar files of indictments and various associated documents, but for the period before 1607 they survive only for the Home Circuit. The Home Circuit indictments have been calendared by county for the reigns of Elizabeth I and James I.[23] The survival of the assize courts' files gradually improves through time. Unfortunately, the associated depositions – potentially useful for the evidence of a social nature which they provide – have also had a poor survival rate and only those for the Northern Circuit are extant for the early-modern period. Analysis of the crimes which came before the assize judges shows that burglary, housebreaking and petty theft were the most common offences in towns. The various categories of homicide generally constituted fewer than 10 per cent of their cases. They also dealt with such matters as treason, forgery and slander. As this summary suggests, there was some overlap between the jurisdiction of the justices of the peace and the assize judges and court of King's Bench.

More evidence of a social, economic and topographical nature was generated by litigation than through criminal proceedings. The civil actions brought in the common law courts of King's Bench, Common Pleas and Exchequer are recorded on the plea rolls. Those for King's

Bench are in class KB 27 until 1702, when the distinction was made between the crown books, containing criminal actions, and the plea or judgement books, which thereafter form classes KB 28 and KB 122 respectively. Those of the Common Pleas are in CP 40 and of the Exchequer, which was less used than either of the other two courts, in E 13. Some cases that were begun in the Westminster courts were transferred to the assize judges under the *nisi prius* procedure and heard locally by them, but there are comparatively few papers for such actions for the early-modern period, partly because the records were commonly returned to the courts in which the action had been initiated. Actions begun in one of the common law courts may also have been heard in another court, albeit with a different slant, for some defendants brought counter-actions. A dispute over the payment of rent, the terms of the tenure and the allowances to be made by Gerard Wayman for the cost of improvements undertaken by his tenant Charles, Lord Granville, to a house in Soho Square, was aired when Wayman sued his lordship in the Common Pleas. In 1694 the same case was heard in Chancery, with Granville as complainant and Wayman as the indignant defendant, grumbling that the house was actually 'much dampnified' because of the alterations, which are detailed in a schedule of their cost.[24] Similarly, suits in Chancery or the other equity courts could be transferred to the common law courts and heard before a jury.

Granville versus Wayman is not untypical of the kind of case that came before the equity courts. Equity had grown up alongside the common law, from which it had developed, and it never had an existence wholly independent of it. A sixteenth-century writer observed that one who was 'without remedie in the common lawe' could take a case to Chancery and there seek redress 'according to equitie and reason'.[25] This was the basis of the popularity of the equity courts, which attracted a great deal of business. Chancery was the oldest and the busiest of them. Exchequer's equity side only developed in the course of the sixteenth century; the third such court, Requests, was a prerogative court which originated in the late fifteenth century and was, like Star Chamber, an offshoot of the Privy Council. Requests ceased to operate at the outbreak of the Civil War and was never revived. The nature of the cases heard varied little between the three courts, although Requests was intended to be one to which the poor could have ready access.

There seems to have been no limit to the issues which could lead to litigation, involving both individuals and corporate bodies, and as a result many aspects of urban life were aired during the proceedings of these courts. Three kinds of cases useful to urban historians may serve to illustrate the kind of material produced. These can be broadly categorized as relating to contract, the disposal of a deceased person's estate and custom.

Contract cases included breaches of the terms of a lease, the non-payment of rent or the full purchase price of a property, or perhaps the failure to complete a building or its repair. The terms of a lease, purchase contract or building agreement are commonly to be found amongst the evidence submitted. Such building agreements are particularly useful for identifying the organization of the building trade and the costs of house construction, with the proportions of the various elements. Papers in a case in Exchequer give the bills for a house built in Deal in 1803, the total cost of which was £853 17s. 0½d., all but £68 1s. 11¾d. of this being for carpentry, bricklaying and plastering.[26] Other contracts not fulfilled included those by which trade and industry were financed. There is a great deal of information in the equity courts' papers relating to internal trade, from which its geographical pattern and the structure of its organization and finance can be traced. Contracts presented as evidence show how, for example, the London brewers were supplied by the maltsters in the counties around the capital.[27] Internal trade of this kind was based upon a complex system of credit and it was when this began to break down that cases of default were brought before the courts. Cases also arose in the event of fraudulent dealings coming to light, or when business partnerships were dissolved, revealing the network of business contracts in operation and the extent to which kinship played a part in such networks.

Family relationships are also shown in those cases which derived from disputes arising from wills, perhaps with the executors challenged on their interpretation of the testator's intentions or because of intestacy. Such suits could become complex, time consuming and expensive, especially if there were a number of claimants upon the estate or if landed property was involved. A classic example of this kind which has been unravelled concerned the heirs of Robert Baker of Piccadilly Hall, a haberdasher who, having accumulated a considerable estate in London's West End, died in 1623 leaving a will, a widow and five children. Nevertheless, because of the death of all these children within the next ten years, claimants to his estate fought each other in the courts for much of the remainder of the century, chiefly in Chancery but with occasional forays into King's Bench, Common Pleas and Exchequer. A final decision came in 1681, but the beneficiary died only a few days later, having in any case been forced to sell much of the estate to finance the actions in support of his claim.[28] This was the kind of case parodied so memorably by Charles Dickens as Jarndyce versus Jarndyce in his novel *Bleak House* (1852–3). The nature of a deceased's estate and the circle of his kin and business contacts are revealed by such disputes, which may also provide evidence for social customs, such as age of marriage.

Changes of custom which led to a dispute coming before the equity courts typically involved clashes over rights, with one party alleged to have altered an established practice in, for instance, usurping the right of appointment to a post, or to collect dues or tolls. Many customary disputes of interest to urban historians relate to fairs and markets, in terms of the arrangements by which tolls were levied, the physical environment, those who were trading and the economy of the town. Some of these were internal, between conflicting interests within a town, and others were external, brought by towns against others which were threatening their position. Early in Elizabeth's reign the citizens of Bath took a complaint to the Court of Requests against the new wool market at Marshfield, six miles away, alleging that the inhabitants there had taken advantage of an epidemic at Bath to establish the new market, in addition to its long-standing rights, attracting the country people to it and away from Bath.[29] At St Neots, Huntingdonshire, a dispute erupted in the early seventeenth century after the local squire had railed and paved the market place and begun to levy tolls for the use of it. His son had to defend a suit brought by a combination of farmers from nearby and citizens of the town, who all objected to paying the tolls. Similar tolls were still being taken there 70 years later when another dispute was provoked by the refusal of a corn chandler and merchant of the town to pay them on specified quantities of corn and other produce. The nature of his trade and that of the town are described, as is the effect of the extension of the navigation of the River Ouse earlier in the century, which had brought increased and more varied commerce to St Neots, including some overseas trade, notably in Polish grain and Norwegian timber. It had also had a physical impact, with stalls and shops erected in the market place and storehouses and warehouses built in the town. Similar topographical information is given in other cases. A rather complex dispute which was concerned with the markets and fairs, chief rents and the election of officers at Shaftesbury gives the names of the inns around the market place there.[30] Inns feature in many descriptions of marketing and trade in cases before the courts, because of their important role in internal commerce.

Inherent in disputes respecting custom was a retrospective element, with one party trying to establish that the other had brought about a change, so that the previous practices were described, together with the current situation, to draw the contrast. Unfortunately, the material is not always easy to interpret. Both sides were supported by witnesses who made sworn depositions to prepared questions, producing evidence of considerable bulk and complexity. The statements made by the witnesses for the plaintiffs are likely to conflict somewhat from those in support of the defendants, but in some cases they are so flatly contradictory that it is difficult to disentangle the inconsistencies of the claims and arrive at a picture which can be confidently regarded as approaching the truth of the matter. This is especially so if there are no decrees or orders of the court to provide some guidance through the minefield of opposing statements. Yet, even if the facts of a case cannot be unravelled satisfactorily, much can often be drawn from the evidence in terms of non-contentious statements, or details which were mentioned, perhaps almost incidentally to the point at issue. The identities of the principals and the deponents may be useful, for it was common for their trades or statuses, addresses and ages to be noted and so it should be possible to compile a kind of cast list of persons involved in a case. From the evidence presented in a dispute over the sheep market at Banbury in the 1650s, 86 men and women can be identified.[31] Examination of such a list may reveal a pattern which can be explained with reference to other information. It may be, for example, that the members of rival cliques within a town lined up on opposite sides in a dispute which was not ostensibly concerned with the nature of the division between them. The testimonies of witnesses may be more readily understood if their allegiances are known.

The general procedure in equity was for a bill to be submitted on behalf of the plaintiff which the defendant could demur, that is, claim that the allegations did not warrant the intervention of the court, or which he or she could deny, or, as a third course, the defendant could question the jurisdiction. Witnesses were examined after the defendant had submitted an answer, and finally the court issued a decree or order in the case. The bills and answers, depositions, and decrees and orders which were produced represent a mass of material to which access can be gained through a series of indices and calendars, with varying degrees of difficulty, depending upon the court and the date of the suit being searched for. The prior knowledge of the names of the plaintiff and defendant is a clear advantage when approaching the Public Record Office's various and varied guides to the courts' papers. Searches for material on a particular town are generally more difficult and for some classes, such as those of the Chancery proceedings after 1714, there is no geographical index to the cases. The most readily accessible classes are the bills and orders, depositions, and decrees and orders in Exchequer (E 111–12, E 133–4, E 123–7), Chancery proceedings and depositions before 1714 (C 1–10, C 21–2, C 24) and the papers of the Court of Requests until the end of Elizabeth's reign (REQ 2).

The equity courts handled a great many cases. This was particularly true of Chancery, which reputedly had 23,000 causes before it in 1653. It became notorious for the slowness of its proceedings and the expense of cases which it heard. By the early nineteenth century it was apparent that something had to be done to improve this state of affairs, and between 1831 and 1858 a number of reforms were instituted. Changes were also effected in the operation of some of the other central courts during the early Victorian period, most notably in 1842, when Exchequer's equity jurisdiction was transferred to Chancery. More comprehensive reforms were produced by the Judicature Acts of 1873 and 1875, which implemented many of the recommendations of the royal commission on the administration of justice that had been established in 1867. These Acts created the High Court of Justice, which absorbed the functions of the courts of Queen's Bench, Common Pleas, Exchequer, Chancery, Admiralty, Probate, Divorce and Matrimonial Causes, which thereby ceased to operate. The assize courts survived these reforms and were abolished by the 1971 Courts Act.

## Charity Commissions

Late Elizabethan legislation gave the Lord Chancellor, or the Lord Keeper, the authority to investigate charities from time to time, and to correct abuses by decree. The decrees could be queried by exceptions submitted by the parties involved and depositions of evidence were taken. The inquisitions, decrees, confirmations and exceptions, and depositions are in the Chancery records in classes C 90, C 91 and C 93. The procedure generated detailed material on local charities, including almshouses and schools. The commissioners were concerned with the details of administration as well as the implementation of benefactors' wishes, even including such matters as the vexed question of teachers' pay. Following a decree in Chancery in 1615 the salary of the master of Warwick school was doubled, and four years later a decree concerning Nuneaton school commented that the annual stipend of £20 was 'noe sufficient wages' for the master there. The reports of the Charity Commissions appointed periodically during the early nineteenth century are also informative on the terms, history and operation of local charities. They show that in some instances the terms of an endowment were not fulfilled. It was discovered in 1827, for example, that although the terms of the will of John Milward, proved in 1654, provided funds for an exhibition for scholars from Birmingham Grammar School to attend Brasenose College, in fact none had ever been sent.[32] In 1853 the Charity Commission was established on a permanent basis and, in addition to further reports, it maintained a register of trusts. The Commission retains its own records.

# Chapter Eight
# CULTURE AND LEISURE

One aspect of the early-modern town which made it distinct from the surrounding countryside in the eyes of contemporaries was its separate culture. This was a difference which was carefully nurtured by the citizens, who sought to maintain that 'civility'. It was especially marked in ceremonies conducted by the corporation and guild companies, which emphasized their constitutional independence. Urban culture was partly a product of such self-conscious separateness, and also partly the result of a concentration of population and the role of a town as a gathering place for citizens and country people on market and fair days. A new dimension was added to urban social life when, in the second half of the seventeenth century, the county gentry, who had hitherto kept largely aloof from the towns, began to move into them for at least a part of the year. The same period also saw the beginnings of the emergence from the growing professional classes of a landless, or pseudo, urban gentry. These processes helped to bring a more commercial element to organized leisure activities, such as balls, concerts, the theatre and horse racing, as well as to cock-fighting and bull-baiting, which also received the gentry's support.[1] It may, too, have served to accentuate the contrast between polite and popular culture, between the world of the coffee-house and that of the alehouse. The latter came under attack from time to time as the civic authorities attempted to curb what they saw as the excesses produced by the more turbulent celebrations of holidays, as well as general lawlessness.

In the late eighteenth and early nineteenth centuries there was a change in the patterns of working-class leisure because of such pressures from authority, and also as a result of a decline in the number of holidays. The Bank of England's closed days are an indication of this trend: they fell from 47 in the mid eighteenth century to 40 in 1825 and then abruptly to only four in 1834.[2] This process reflected increased industrialization and the needs of factory owners for planned and maximized production, which led, too, to the regular working day. The period was also one of decline for many traditional pastimes, partly for these reasons and partly because, as towns grew and became more densely occupied, so the amount of recreational space was reduced. Only later in the nineteenth century did some of these pastimes reappear as formalized sports. Much day-to-day leisure activity in the nineteenth and early twentieth centuries was centred on the pubs, working mens' clubs and mechanics' institutes, the churches and chapels, and societies for a wide range of activities, including music, which was an important cultural element in urban society. In addition, the process by which the number of holidays had fallen was slowly reversed and a growing proportion of the population was able to enjoy a break from work. One consequence of such increased leisure time and the greater ease and speed of travel produced by the railways was that seaside spas and watering places, established primarily for the relaxation of the gentry and professional classes, were transformed into popular resorts. The nineteenth century also saw a growing provision for working-class recreation by philanthropic interests and the civic authorities.

There were other changes. Some towns lost their fairs, which fell into abeyance or were deliberately suppressed because of their more boisterous aspects. Towns which had benefited from the gentry's patronage were abandoned by them, although others, particularly the country market towns, continued to enjoy their custom. Despite such changes, towns retained their distinct cultural identities, providing facilities which the villages were unable to sustain, such as baths and washhouses, music halls, theatres, picture palaces, concert halls and football league clubs.

## Civic records

Civic ceremonial was focused especially upon the annual mayoral inauguration, which was typically an elaborate affair that consisted of prayers offered by the councillors for guidance, the formal selection of the mayor, a church service, a banquet and the taking of the oath by the new mayor, either as part of these ceremonies or shortly afterwards. These events marked the beginning of a new civic year, with appointments also made to other corporation offices. Sometimes, although rarely, this date was altered, as it was at Coventry in 1556, when it was moved from 2 February to 1 November. In the aftermath of the Reformation civic authorities tended to switch the emphasis of their ceremonial events away from that half of the year in which the religious feasts fall – that is, from 25 December to 24 June – to the secular half.[3] The mayoral inauguration was mentioned in council minutes because of its significance, but other regular festivities, such as those held to commemorate the Restoration, the anniversaries of the defeat of the Armada and the Gunpowder Plot, or the monarch's birthday, may only be minuted if it was necessary to cancel them for some reason, such as an outbreak of plague. Special celebrations were more likely to be discussed by the council, if only to fix the date and nature of the events and perhaps to note decisions on how they should be financed. The arrangements for visits of a royal or noble retinue may be described in some detail. The costs of such occasional events should appear in the accounts; those of the regular annual celebrations may be entered individually or subsumed in a fixed sum set aside to pay for such entertainments. The expense of retaining a band of municipal musicians, or waits, should also be recorded.

Another characteristic civic ceremony was the annual perambulation of the boundaries by the mayor, aldermen, councillors, members of the guilds, churchmen and various other citizens, perhaps in a generally sober state, perhaps not. They were serenaded by the waits on such occasions. As with other regular civic events, the actual form of the perambulation was not described in the records unless there was cause to review it and perhaps to correct undesirable practices which had crept in. At Oxford the annual 'riding of the franchises' included a boat trip to cover that part of the boundaries which ran along the river and this led to some problems in the later seventeenth century. In 1680 it was ordered that the musicians should sit 'at the end of Mr. Mayor's Boate and play all Dinner while as hath been accustomed' and only councillors and their guests should enter that boat, instead of the recent improper practice whereby the freemen generally had been 'pressing into the Mayor's boat' so that the musicians could not play there. Another indignity which had arisen was that those who accompanied the procession had got into the habit of immoderately splashing the mayor and councillors with water. A more serious incident occurred during the particularly dirty parliamentary election campaign of 1696, when the mayor's and the chamberlains' boats were stopped and their occupants threatened with violence while they were ceremonially touring the boundaries.[4] It is through the council's attempts to end such irregularities during one of its major annual events that a picture of the event itself emerges.

The members of the guild companies also contributed to the distinctive urban culture, for they both participated in the civic ceremonials and held their own round of dinners and processions, which mirrored those of the corporation. They, too, celebrated their annual elections of officers and other regular feast days, and if one of their members was chosen to high civic office they did not miss the opportunity to mark the occasion in an appropriate manner. Their minute books and accounts provide similar information to those of the corporations. With the decline in their regulation of trades in the eighteenth century some guilds dissolved, but others survived, largely as 'convivial societies' which continued to hold their periodic feasts.[5] In 1784 there were 112 guests at the annual dinner of the tailors' guild at Lincoln, celebrating 'with the greatest mirth and friendship'.[6] In much the same way, civic culture emerged from the nineteenth-century reorganizations without too many changes, for the new reformed corporations adopted similar regalia and ceremonial customs to those of their predecessors and followed much the same round of banquetings and other engagements.[7]

From the mid nineteenth century municipal authorities began to make provision for working-class leisure, setting aside space for parks and erecting public libraries, baths and washhouses. This was often done with the help of public subscriptions and perhaps in combination with private benefactors, such as Andrew Carnegie, who financed the building of many public libraries in the early twentieth century. Civic museums, art galleries and concert halls were also provided, drawing a largely middle-class clientele. Local government records contain the evidence for the erection of such buildings and their subsequent maintenance and usage, with attendance statistics and details, such as the numbers of book issues at libraries, arranged by subject. Separate committees were created to deal with libraries, parks, entertainments, museums and art galleries, and baths and washhouses. The dates when such committees were formed can be regarded as marking a council's commitment to the provision of those facilities, and their records and reports may supply more details than the council's minutes and accounts.

Corporation records also provide information on popular events, partly because of attempts to prohibit or regulate those which were celebrated in a rather vigorous manner. The civic authorities increasingly distanced themselves from popular festivals. In 1726 the council at Preston withdrew from the bull-baiting held in the town because it had proved impossible to restrain 'the turbulent and unruly passions of the common people'.[8] The annual bull-running at Wokingham in Berkshire was a major event in the civic calendar, presided over by the mayor and corporation, but this, too, tended to get out of hand, with the bull-running followed by street brawls which in 1808 had a tragic outcome, for the parish register records that 'Martha May, aged 55 (who was hurt by fighters after bull-baiting) was buried December 31st'. This event gradually fell into disfavour and came to an end early in Victoria's reign.[9] References to sporting fatalities do occur from time to time in the burial registers and coroners' inquests.

Prohibitions of such rumbustious activities are recorded in the council and court minutes. A number of towns attempted to stop the playing of football in the streets, for example. In 1608 the court leet at Manchester banned it, apparently because the inhabitants were 'greatlye wronged and charged with makinge and amendinge of their glasse windowes broken yearlye and spoyled by a companye of lewde and disordered persons'.[10] By the early nineteenth century football was more or less suppressed as an urban sport, but it reappeared later in the century as a formal and regulated game. Other games died out and did not reappear. These included blood sports, such as cock-fighting. Norwich corporation banned bonfires in the streets, unless permission had been obtained from the mayor.[11] Those caught breaching such regulations in too flagrant a manner appeared before the civic courts and the records of such cases can provide useful insights into the kinds of incidents which occurred on festival days. They also reveal the tensions between the polite civic celebrations on the one hand and the more boisterous merrymakings of the majority of the population on the other. On 5 November 1670 a bonfire was made in the street outside Alderman Butler's house in Exeter and a weaver and a servant were brought before the city sessions a few days later accused of throwing fireworks into the alderman's doorway.[12] Their rather provocative way of celebrating that holiday contrasted with the corporation's more dignified feastings. Tensions also arose when a predominantly puritan magistracy attempted to suppress such popular traditional revelry as dancing around the maypole. In Coventry the maypoles were removed in 1591 and similar moves at Leicester in 1599 and 1603 caused much dispute. The attempts to remove the maypole at Banbury in 1588 and 1589 led to disturbances which were drawn to the Privy Council's attention, as was the corporation's arrest of a group of strolling actors as 'wandering rogues' in 1633.[13] Star Chamber's concern with riots extended to those which occurred during popular revelries. In a case before the court relating to an uproar at Weymouth in 1570 it was deposed that in the spring it was the practice in the town and neighbourhood on 'Sundays and other holydaies . . . to electe and chuse one of the said inhabitants to be Robin Hoode and another Lyttell John, which persons have bin appointed for the Trayninge and Enstructinge of the youth with divers kinds of activity and vertuous exercises'.[14]

Much of the regular social activity in towns was centred on the inns and alehouses. These were licensed and the records of the justices of the peace should supply information from which their numbers and distribution can be plotted. Inns tended to be concentrated in the town centres, around the market places. The alehouses, on the other hand, were generally to be found in the poorer quarters. There were intermittent attempts by the magistrates in most towns to clamp down on the unlicensed alehouses and prosecute their keepers. In 1629 Oxford corporation thought that there were in the town 'a multitude of Alehowses and most of them unlycensed' and it tried to limit the number; in 1642 this was set at 89, but the true figure was much higher, as it was difficult to enforce the licensing procedure.[15] Alehouses were the focus of the 'alternative society' and the nefarious activities carried on within them attracted the attention of the magistrates. Cases in the civic courts indicate the social status of those who frequented the alehouses and the games, licit and illicit, which were played there.[16] Some of the depositions in such cases are rather inconsequential, providing only a partial glimpse into the everyday popular culture of the citizens. Even so, they may have some interest. An example from Nottingham records that in August 1688 two men drinking together fell to quarrelling 'about their Learning' which resulted in one of them, who was rather drunk, betting the other 'that he could not take a Greeke verse and turne it into Lattin, and after that into English'. Unfortunately, the outcome of this intriguing and imaginative wager was not recorded.[17]

## Antiquarians, travellers and diarists

Antiquarians commonly recorded the principal cultural events in the towns which they studied. This partly reflected civic pride and an awareness that they were an integral part of the urban identity, and partly a realization that some of those ceremonies which they witnessed were in decline and might not survive, which indeed was often the case. Stebbing Shaw, the historian of Staffordshire, included a detailed description of the 'Whitsun Bower' ceremony at Lichfield in his *History and Antiquities* of the county, published in 1798. The same event had been noted by Celia Fiennes a century earlier. Indeed, travellers' journals like hers are a further source, for both popular rites and civic ceremonies. Thomas Baskerville visited Norwich in 1681 and noted that in the town hall 'the mayor and his brethren with the livery men of this city keep a great feast, presenting the ladies that come thither with marchpanes [marzipans] to carry away. They have also fine shows in the streets, in some measure like that of the Lord Mayor's Day of London . . . the mayor and his brethren . . . richly clad in their scarlet robes'.[18]

Daniel Defoe was concerned more with economic life than with ceremonial, but he was anxious about the moral effects of some features of genteel urban society which he recognized while on his tour. He deplored the 'assemblies among the younger gentry' such as he found at York 'as a plan laid for the ruin of the nation's morals'. There was, he noted, an 'abundance of good families' in that city. His opinion of Bury St Edmunds was similar. It was 'thronged with gentry, people of the best fashion, and the most polite conversation' and 'the beauty of this town consists of the number of gentry who dwell in and near it'. There were 'abundance of the finest ladies' at the assemblies there, but Defoe disapproved of 'the scandalous liberty some take at these assemblèes'.[19] The gentry society which he found at York, Bury St Edmunds and elsewhere was often separate from that of the urban elite and also physically distinct from it, with the town houses of the gentry concentrated in particular districts. This was most marked in London's contrasting West End and City, which the dramatists portrayed as a divergence between the West End's sophisticated but penurious young aristocrats and gentry and the plodding, gullible, yet wealthy, City merchants. This was deliberate overstatement, of course, but something of a similar contrast between these elements could be identified in other cities and towns where the gentry formed a separate social group. It was not unusual for there to be a social distinction between a cathedral close and the remainder of a city. This was the case at Worcester, where the Cathedral Green − an enclave of county jurisdiction within the city's boundaries − attracted the county gentry, a feature which is apparent from the hearth tax and poll tax returns.[20] There was a similar pattern at Lincoln, for the Bail and the Close on the hill around the cathedral were part of the shire and the district where the county families had their houses, separated both physically and socially from the citizens 'below-hill', few of whom were able to make the transition up the hill.[21] There was not always such a marked geographical separation of the gentry from the other citizens and some small towns became more or less gentrified in the late seventeenth and eighteenth centuries. This applied to Warwick, for example, where the rebuilding after a major fire in 1694 produced a town centre of a rather different social, as well as physical, composition from the one which had been destroyed. Even some small market towns attracted reputations for social pretension. Hingham, 12 miles from Norwich, was regarded in this way in the eighteenth century: the antiquarian Francis Blomefield quoted a remark that 'the inhabitants are taken notice of as a gentile sort of people, so fashionable in their dress that the town is called by the neighbours "Little-London"'.[22]

The cultural life which the gentry brought to such towns can be glimpsed through their correspondence, which describes, amongst the tittle tattle, the kind of social events which were held and the nature of the company that attended them. The events were typically balls, dinners, masquerades, plays, concerts and horse races. The most notable guests were singled out for a mention in such correspondence. A letter of 31 August 1696 reported that at Bath 'there were balls every night' and at the one held on that particular evening were 'the Earl of Kingston and Lord Brookes and Lord Clifford and Lord Coningsby and Lady Wharton and several other great persons . . .'.[23] The town was then well on the way to becoming the pre-eminent spa, a position which it held throughout the eighteenth century. The most important events attracted considerable numbers, especially during the season, in the spas and larger towns. In 1788 the diarist James Woodforde, parson of Weston Longeville, Norfolk, spent two days at Norwich, on the first of which he was in an audience of 900 at a 'Miscellaneous Concert'; on the second he attended a performance of Handel's "Judas Maccabeus" at St Peter's church, together with perhaps as many as 1,200 others. He passed an enjoyable, if rather expensive, couple of days, but, perhaps most importantly, he had been to a major social occasion attended by 'Almost all of the principal Families in the County'.[24]

The spas developed because their spring water attracted visitors seeking to improve·their health, but they also became places of resort for those who could afford to mix in the distinctive and exclusive type of society which they produced. From the mid–eighteenth century, seaside towns began to experience the same kind of popularity, as watering places for the aristocracy, gentry and professional classes. In 1778 Margate was said to be 'adorned with houses fit for the reception of people of the first rank' and in 1810 it was 'crowded with company, and indeed may be considered as London in miniature'.[25] Brighton and Weymouth both enjoyed royal patronage. The increase in leisure time and prosperity among the middle classes and the growing popularity of sea bathing widened the social appeal of the resorts. This was a process commented upon by Southey, who thought that the visitors were influenced chiefly by fashion, 'not the desirableness of the accommodations, not the convenience of the shore for their ostensible purpose, bathing' and so they were 'capricious; they frequent a coast some seasons in succession, then desert it for some other . . .'.[26] The coming of the railways from the 1840s onwards wrought a greater transformation, making seaside holidays and day excursions available to a considerable and expanding section of the urban population. Not only were coastal towns and villages developed into resorts, but new seaside towns were created by the holiday trade. To the correspondence and diaries describing the holidaymakers' adventures were added their pithy remarks sent on picture postcards, which themselves reveal something of the nature of a resort.[27]

## Guide books

The guide book is one of the major sources for the study of resorts. The earliest ones were issued in the mid eighteenth century and their subsequent development and popularity owed a great deal to the improvements in communications and the growth of the holiday trade, although they were also produced for visitors to inland towns and cities which did not have specific holiday functions. By the mid nineteenth century the guide book had become a distinctive and successful type of publication, with frequent editions issued for most resorts.

Many aspects of a resort's character, and perhaps its changing role, can be identified from its guide books. Scarborough was able to make the transition from a spa to a holiday resort, and provided for clientele from a number of sections of society in different parts of the town.[28] Elsewhere a marked social distinction between neighbouring resorts can be recognized. On the Lancashire coast sedate St Annes contrasted with Blackpool, which from its early days was a largely working-class resort, although with a 'better end' at its North Shore. In the mid twentieth century St Annes still represented 'a citadel of middle class respectability where boarding houses style themselves private hotels and serve dinner – that infallible social symbol – rather than the high tea of Blackpool'.[29] The object of a guide book was to project a resort in a favourable light, so that its description of the place tended to be complimentary, if not actually eulogistic. In addition to such descriptions and well-chosen illustrations, guide books carried much practical information for the visitor, such as coaching – and later, railway – timetables, lists of hotels and boarding houses and accounts of the various attractions, facilities and events. They drew attention to the charms to be found on the pier, that distinguishing, if not always distinguished, feature of seaside resorts. The advertisements are almost equally informative. A long series of guide books for a resort is revealing in respect of, for example, the changing kind of accommodation available and perhaps of the types of visitors which were catered for.[30]

Other sources provide fuller evidence on a resort's economy. Census returns, ratebooks and directories carry information on social zoning and the extent to which there was a specialized holiday industry. They may present an incomplete picture, however, partly because the holiday trade was seasonal and so for many households only a supplementary source of income. The reports of the medical officer of health for Blackpool show that both the censuses and the directories under-recorded the numbers of landladies there.[31] Censuses can also be used to establish the age, sex and social profile of visitors, but again they are not ideal for the purpose, and the time of the year when the census was taken has to be considered in interpreting the results. The 1841 census, taken in June, is hardly comparable with that for 1851, which was taken at the end of March, so far as visitors to seaside resorts are concerned.[32]

Guide books give prominence to buildings providing public entertainment, which typically included assembly rooms, theatres, newsrooms and libraries, concert halls, ballrooms and, later, picture palaces and cinemas. The spas were among the earliest towns to provide buildings of this kind. At Bath, the first playhouse opened in 1705, the Pump Room in the following year, the Assembly Rooms in 1708 and the Ballroom in 1720. Many towns acquired such buildings in the course of the eighteenth century. Assembly rooms, which could be adapted as a theatre, were erected in Leicester around 1750, 20 years after Lincoln's first theatre had opened. Theatres were not restricted to the larger towns, however, for their popularity extended beyond the patronage of the gentry, and they were established in 13 other Lincolnshire towns during the eighteenth century, including such small ones as Alford and Market Deeping.[33] Some theatres were attached to inns and so may not be marked on town plans, which in other respects are a useful source for identifying public buildings. Other features shown on town plans which are evidence for the leisured pastimes of the citizens and visitors are pleasure gardens, bowling greens and race courses. Such plans were included in many guide books and were also published separately in a form which the visitors would find convenient, incorporating appropriate information for their use.

## Newspapers and ephemera

Provincial newspapers were first published in the early eighteenth century. There were 24 in existence in 1723 and 35 by 1760, but these figures conceal a complex picture, for the numbers of papers fluctuated considerably and some had a very short existence.[34] Stability eventually followed this early volatility and more towns came to be served by a regular, usually weekly, local paper. The style and size of such newspapers changed considerably during the nineteenth century, and especially after the removal of the taxes on them and on paper between 1855 and 1861. Thereafter the number of titles increased rapidly. The papers became larger, carrying more news and advertisements, and local daily papers began to appear.

The advertisements are particularly interesting for their evidence on the range of goods and services available. Tailors, milliners, haberdashers, drapers, watchmakers, wig-makers, booksellers and numerous other tradespeople advertised their wares, drawing the readers' attention to their luxury items and the fashions newly arrived from London. A considerable increase in the availability of such goods in the course of the eighteenth century should be apparent. This evidence is not in any way a representative profile of the kinds of tradesmen in a town, however, for many did not advertise. It was the purveyors of luxury goods who were most likely to place newspaper advertisements, some of which were quite elaborate. Dancing-masters, language and music tutors, schools and academies also advertised, indicating the nature of the education and social instruction which could be obtained. The schools and academies commonly itemized the subjects that were taught and mentioned their charges.

Social events and the meetings of various organizations are also noticed in the papers. Much urban cultural life from the early eighteenth century onwards was centred on clubs, associations and societies. In the Georgian town there were clubs for a whole range of purposes and serving virtually all sections of society. Their most obvious common feature was their conviviality; meetings were generally held in inns and taverns. Such clubs did not survive long into the nineteenth century, which was characterized rather by more orderly societies, both recreational and instructional in nature. They included the temperance societies and improvement associations established largely by the middle classes to counteract what they saw as the evil effects of excessive drinking. Many societies, indeed much urban cultural life, were affiliated with the churches and chapels. Some organizations were ephemeral and left little, if any, evidence. The lists in guidebooks and directories are useful, but provide only snapshots of those societies that were in existence at the time of compilation and even so may not be complete. The purposes or subjects of the societies are usually obvious from their titles, but not the type or range of membership, or their popularity. Some were socially or intellectually selective, for example, and their rules deliberately restricted the numbers of members. The Clifton Antiquarian Club at Bristol had a maximum of 50 ordinary and 10 honorary members, for instance.[35] Others had a wider membership and a broader purpose. Much can be discovered from their rules, which may have survived amongst their papers. The rules of literary and scientific societies of the mid-Victorian period, that took advantage of the Act of 1843 allowing them exemption from rates by obtaining a certificate from the Barrister for Friendly Societies, should be deposited amongst the clerk of the peace's papers. The newspapers carry notices of meetings and other events, such as public lectures, organized by the societies. They may also have reports describing such occasions and the names of the officers and guests. The reports may provide some indication of the extent of public support for a society by referring to the size of its membership and the numbers attending its meetings.

Newspapers also have announcements of public entertainments, such as balls, routs, concerts, lectures, plays and sporting events. They provide a good idea of the range of such entertainments that were available. The kinds of music and choral societies that were active locally should emerge from them, for example. They may also reveal patterns in terms of the types of concert and the nature of the repertoire which was performed. Much fuller information is shown on handbills and posters than is carried in newspaper announcements. They describe the full programme of an event and list those taking part. Playbills typically give a synopsis and cast list of the chief play, with slightly briefer details of the prologue and afterpiece or farce, mention the songs and interludes and perhaps hint at the special effects, leaving the reader full of admiration for the versatility of the actors and the stamina of the audience. Political and reform meetings were similarly advertised in the newspapers and on handbills, showing the extent to which national issues were attracting attention, and the local ones which were arousing interest. A sign of the changing social mores of the early nineteenth century is the bill publicizing a meeting called in 1810 by some inhabitants of north London to consider 'the most effectual Means to prevent the Practice of indecent Bathing in the New River' which apparently had 'long been highly indecent and offensive'. It mentioned the case of a man who 'was found offending by bathing and exposing his Person in the Fields between Islington and Stoke Newington'.[36] The survival rate of bills, posters, theatre, concert and sporting programmes, magazines, pamphlets and other ephemera has not been great, but collections of them do exist and they may also turn up amongst private papers.

Collective leisure time pursuits are, of course, easier to identify than are those of individuals or families. Evenings spent in the pub, or at home sewing, or playing cards or the piano leave little trace in the records, other than in diaries, journals and personal correspondence, and these tend to relate the unusual rather than the familiar and mundane. Some evidence of the extent of music making at home comes from the presence of keyboard and other instruments in probate inventories for the sixteenth, seventeenth and eighteenth centuries, and of pianos in photographs of late-Victorian and Edwardian interiors. This, as with so much evidence, may not be entirely representative and is certainly slanted in terms of social class. Obviously, the routine lives of the population are easier to infer than actually to establish, in terms of both work and leisure. Little remains for posterity from the interests and activities of the vast majority of people. Fortunately for the researcher, antiquarians are an exception and much of their work is available, in manuscript or in print, however uncertain they may themselves have been of the value of their labours. As John Duncumb wrote in the preface to his history of Hereford, which formed the first two volumes of his study of the county, 'The Compiler is well aware that many imperfections will be discernable; some from the difficulties unavoidably incident to the undertaking, and more from his own inability to do justice to a work which embraces subjects of considerable variety . . .'.[37]

# NOTES

## Chapter 1 (pp. 9–20)

1 Charles Gross, *A Bibliography of British Municipal History*, Longman, Green, New York, 1897, p. xxv.
2 W.G. Hoskins, *The Age of Plunder*, Longman, 1976, p. 14.
   Peter Clark and Paul Slack, *English Towns in Transition 1500–1700*, Oxford University Press, 1976, p. 11.
   P.J. Corfield, *The Impact of English Towns 1700–1800*, Oxford University Press, 1982, pp. 2, 7–9.
3 P.J. Waller, *Town, City, and Nation 1850–1914*, Oxford University Press, 1983, pp. 6–8.
4 Robert Tittler, 'The Incorporation of Boroughs, 1540–1558', *History*, vol. 62, 1977, pp. 24–42.
5 Corfield, 1982 op.cit., p. 149.
6 *The Records of the Corporation of Leicester*, Leicester Museums and Art Gallery, 1956, p. 3.
7 Charles John Palmer, ed., Henry Manship, *The History of Great Yarmouth*, Meall, Great Yarmouth, 1854, pp. ii–vi.
8 Caesar Caine, ed., *Analecta Eboracensia, or some Remains of the Ancient City of York, collected by . . . Sir Thomas Widdrington*, C.J. Clark and Phillimore, 1897, pp. x–xi.
9 Peter Clark, 'Visions of the Urban Community: Antiquarians and the English City Before 1800' in Derek Fraser and Anthony Sutcliffe, eds., *The Pursuit of Urban History*, Edward Arnold, 1983, pp. 105–24.
10 Felix Hull, *Guide to the Berkshire Record Office*, Berkshire County Council, Reading, 1952, p. 23. Shropshire County Archivist's Report: Accessions June–October 1960, unpublished TS, p. 6.
11 Christopher A. Markham, ed., *The Records of the Borough of Northampton*, I, Northampton, 1898, p. iii.
12 Lucy Toulmin Smith, ed., *The Itinerary of John Leland in England*, 5 vols., Bell, 1906–10. 'Thomas Baskerville's Journeys in England', Historical Manuscripts Commission, *Thirteenth Report, Appendix Part II, Portland II*, H.M.S.O., 1893. Christopher Morris, ed., *The Journeys of Celia Fiennes*, The Cresset Press, 1947. Pat Rogers, ed., Daniel Defoe, *A Tour through the Whole Island of Great Britain*, Penguin, Harmondsworth, 1971.
13 J.J. Cartwright, ed., *The Travels through England of Dr. Richard Pococke*, Camden Soc., new series, vols. xlii, xliv, 1888–9. C. Bruyn Andrews, ed., *The Torrington Diaries*, 4 vols., Eyre & Spottiswoode, 1934–8.
14 Esther Moir, *The Discovery of Britain: the English Tourists 1540–1840*, Routledge & Kegan Paul, 1964.

15  Toulmin Smith, op.cit., I, p. 7.
16  Morris, op.cit., pp. 129, 147–8.
17  J.P. Mayer, ed., Alexis de Tocqueville, *Journeys to England and Ireland*, Faber & Faber, 1958, pp. 98–104.
18  Robert Latham and William Matthews, eds., *The Diary of Samuel Pepys*, 11 vols., Bell & Hyman, 1970–83. Frederick A. Pottle, ed., *Boswell's London Journal 1762–1763*, Heinemann, 1950. Andrew Clark, ed., *The Life and Times of Anthony Wood, antiquary, of Oxford, 1632–1695, described by Himself*, 5 vols., Oxford Historical Society, 1891–1900.
19  Peter Quennell, ed., *Memoirs of William Hickey*, Hutchinson, 1975.
20  George Sturt, *A Small Boy in the Sixties*, Caliban Books, 1977.

## Chapter 2 (pp. 21–32)

1  Ralph Merrifield, *The Roman City of London*, Ernest Benn, 1965, p. 85.
2  Frank Emery, *The Oxfordshire Landscape*, Hodder & Stoughton, 1974, pp. 202–3.
3  Victoria County History (hereafter V.C.H.) *Oxfordshire*, IV, 1979, pp. 475–7.
4  R.A. Skelton, 'Tudor Town Plans in John Speed's *Theatre*', *Archaeological Journal*, vol. 108, 1952, pp. 109–20.
5  The plans are reproduced in *The Counties of Britain: A Tudor Atlas by John Speed*, Pavilion Books, 1988.
6  James Elliot, *The City in Maps: urban mapping to 1900*, British Library, 1987, pp. 47–9. Bristol R.O., Common Council Minute Book, 1659–75, p. 248.
7  John Hutchins, *History and Antiquities of the County of Dorset*, IV, 2nd ed., 1815, p. 75.
8  Daniel Lysons, *The Environs of London*, III, 1795, pp. 447, 474–5.
9  Robin Bush, ed., *Plan of Taunton . . . by John Wood 1840*, Somerset Archaeological & Natural History Soc., 1980.
10  E. Welch, *Southampton Maps from Elizabethan Times*, Southampton Corporation, 1964. Paul Laxton, 'Richard Horwood's Map and the Face of London, 1799–1819', introduction to *The A to Z of Regency London*, London Topographical Soc., 131, 1985, pp. x–xi.
11  J.J. Bagley, *Historical Interpretation 2: Sources of English History 1540 to the Present Day*, Penguin, Harmondsworth, 1971, p. 179.
12  Elliot, op.cit., pp. 44–7.
13  Walter Minchinton, *Life to the City*, Devon Books, Exeter, 1987, pp. 10, 15.
14  J.B. Harley, *Maps for the local historian. A guide to the British sources*, The Standing Conference for Local History, 1972, p. 14.
15  Gwyn Rowley, *British Fire Insurance Plans*, Charles Goad, Hatfield, 1984, pp. 15–17.
16  Ibid, pp. 89–95, has an inventory of the plans, by place.
17  M.D. Lobel, *The Atlas of Historic Towns*, 2, Scolar Press, 1975, Bristol maps 4 and 8.

**Chapter 3 (pp. 33–50)**

1  F. Sheppard and V. Belcher, 'The Deeds Registries of Yorkshire and Middlesex', *Journal of the Society of Archivists*, vol. 6, 1980, pp. 274–86.

2  *Records of the Corporation of Leicester*, p. 24.

3  M.J. Power, 'East London housing in the seventeenth century' in Peter Clark and Paul Slack, eds., *Crisis and order in English towns 1500–1700*, Routledge & Kegan Paul, 1972, pp. 237–62.

4  Gloucestershire R.O., GDR G3/19. Lincolnshire Archives Office, CC 27/7, p. 21.

5  *Gloucester Journal*, 20 September 1743.

6  Peter Thomas and Jacqueline Warren, *Aspects of Exeter*, Jay, Plymouth, 1980, p. 141.

7  V.C.H. *Oxfordshire*, X, 1972, pp. 34–6. Stuart Davies, 'The Rebuilding of a House in Gloucester, 1701–2', *Transactions of the Bristol and Gloucestershire Archaeological Soc.*, vol. 98, 1980, pp. 173–8.

8  *A New Plan of the Town of Nottingham By H. Wild & T.H. Smith*, 1820.

9  Roy Millward, *Lancashire*, Hodder & Stoughton, 1955, p. 86.

10  Asa Briggs, *Victorian Cities*, Penguin, Harmondsworth, 1968, pp. 158–83, 206–7.

11  S. Martin Gaskell, *Building Control: National Legislation and the Introduction of Local Bye-Laws in Victorian England*, Bedford Square Press, 1983.

12  C.C. Knowles and P.H. Pitt, *The History of Building Regulation in London 1189–1972*, Architectural Press, 1972, pp. 37–96.

13  Guildhall Library, London, MS 11,936/26, p. 227. H.A.L. Cockerell and Edwin Green, *The British Insurance Business 1547–1970*, Heinemann, 1976, p. 26.

14  Cockerell and Green, op.cit., p. 28.

15  Guildhall Library, London, MSS 11,936/26, 30, 33.

16  P.G.M. Dickson, *The Sun Insurance Office, 1710–1960*, Oxford University Press, 1960, p. 85.

17  Kent Archives Office, PRC 11/73/213.

18  B.R. Curle, ed., 'Kensington and Chelsea Probate Inventories 1672–1734', unpublished TS, 1970, pp. 89–91.

19  Ursula Priestley and P.J. Corfield, 'Rooms and room use in Norwich housing 1580–1730', *Post Medieval Archaeology*, vol. 16, 1982, pp. 117–20.

20  Paul Hindle, *Maps for Local History*, Batsford, 1988, pp. 81–4.

21  C.F. Slade, 'Topography of the early modern town, c.1500–c.1750' in Michael Reed, ed., *Discovering Past Landscapes*, Croom Helm, 1984, pp. 199–201.

22  P.J. Corfield, *Towns, Trade, Religion and Radicalism: The Norwich Perspective on English History*, University of East Anglia, 1980, pp. 16–17, 37.

**Chapter 4 (pp. 51–68)**

1  Keith Thomas, 'Numeracy in Early Modern England', *Transactions of the Royal Historical Soc.*, 5th series, vol. 37, 1987, pp. 103–32.

2  Charles Phythian-Adams, *Desolation of a City: Coventry and the Urban Crisis of the Late Middle Ages*, Cambridge University Press, 1979, pp. 189–90, 291–3. Robert Tittler, 'The vitality of an Elizabethan port: the economy of Poole, c. 1500–1600', *Southern History*, vol. 7, 1985, p. 96.

3  Ian Roy and Stephen Porter, 'The Social and Economic Structure of an Early Modern Suburb: the Tything at Worcester', *Bulletin of the Institute of Historical Research*, vol. LIII, 1980, pp. 203–17.

4  Lambeth Palace Library, MS 2712, f. 46.

5  John Smith, *Men and Armour for Gloucestershire in 1608*, Sotheran, 1902, p. 1.

6  Allen Chinnery, 'The Muster Roll for Leicester of 1608', *Transactions of the Leicestershire Archaeological and Historical Soc.*, vol. LX, 1986, pp. 25–33.

7  Paul Slack, ed., *Poverty in Early-Stuart Salisbury*, Wiltshire Record Soc., vol. XXXI, 1975, pp. 65–82.

8  John Webb, ed., *Poor Relief in Elizabethan Ipswich*, Suffolk Record Soc., vol. IX, 1966.

9  John F. Pound, ed., *The Norwich Census of the Poor 1570*, Norfolk Record Soc., vol. XL, 1971, pp. 7–21, 43.

10  Rose Graham, ed., *The Chantry Certificates*, Oxfordshire Record Soc., vol. I, 1918, pp. 16–24, 44–8.

11  Ian Roy and Stephen Porter, 'The Population of Worcester in 1646', *Local Population Studies*, no. 28, 1982, p. 37.

12  Paul Slack, 'The Local Incidence of Epidemic Disease: the Case of Bristol 1540–1650' in *The Plague Reconsidered: a new look at its origin and effects in sixteenth and seventeenth century England*, Local Population Studies Supplement, 1977, pp. 55–7.

13  V.C.H. *Oxfordshire*, IV, 1979, p. 82.

14  W.G. Hoskins, 'English Provincial Towns in the Early Sixteenth Century' in *Provincial England*, Macmillan, 1963, pp. 68–85.

15  D.V. Glass, 'Socio-economic status and occupations in the City of London at the end of the seventeenth century' in A.E.J. Hollaender and W. Kellaway, eds., *Studies in London History*, Hodder & Stoughton, 1969, pp. 373–89.

16  Worcester Cathedral Archives, D 261.

17  A.F. Meekings, S. Porter and I. Roy, eds., *The Hearth Tax Collectors' Book for Worcester 1678–1680*, Worcestershire Historical Soc., new series, vol. 11, 1983, p. 39. 'The Staffordshire Hearth Tax' in *Collections for a History of Staffordshire*, William Salt Archaeological Soc., 1923, pp. 140–6.

18  Transcribed in *The Town Maps of Warwick 1610–1851*, prepared by the Record Office and published by the County Museum, undated, p. 4.

19  Elizabeth Ralph and Mary E. Williams, eds., *The Inhabitants of Bristol in 1696*, Bristol Record Soc., vol. XXV, 1968. D.V. Glass, ed., *London*

*Inhabitants within the Walls, 1695*, London Record Soc., vol. 2, 1966. 'The LCC Burns Journal' in Peter Laslett, ed., *The Earliest Classics: Graunt and King*, Gregg International, Farnborough, 1973.

20  E.S. De Beer, ed., *The Diary of John Evelyn*, V, Clarendon Press, Oxford, 1955, p. 214.

21  D.V. Glass, 'Two Papers on Gregory King' in D.V. Glass and D.E.C. Eversley, eds., *Population in History*, Edward Arnold, 1965, pp. 159–220. P. Laslett, 'Mean household size in England since the sixteenth century' in P. Laslett and R. Wall, eds., *Household and Family in Past Time*, Cambridge University Press, 1972, pp. 125–58.

22  E.A. Wrigley and R.S. Schofield, *The Population History of England 1541–1871: A Reconstruction*, Edward Arnold, 1981, pp. 208–18, 448–9, 528–9.

23  Andrew Clark, ed., '*Survey of the Antiquities of the City of Oxford*' composed in *1661–6, by Anthony Wood*, II, Oxford Historical Soc., XV, 1889, p. 220. Idem, *The Life and Times of Anthony Wood, antiquary, of Oxford, 1632–1695, described by Himself*, II, Oxford Historical Soc., XXI, 1892, p. 360.

24  B.M. Berry and R.S. Schofield, 'Age at Baptism in Pre-industrial England', *Population Studies*, XXV, 1971, pp. 453–63.

25  J.T. Krause, 'The changing adequacy of English registration, 1690–1837' in Glass and Eversley, 1965 op.cit., pp. 379–93.

26  Wrigley and Schofield, op.cit., p. 255.

27  M.D. George, *London Life in the Eighteenth Century*, Penguin, Harmondsworth, 1966, p. 398.

28  Historical Manuscripts Commission, *Report on the Records of the City of Exeter*, H.M.S.O., 1916, p. 381.

29  Alan Everitt, 'Country, County and Town: Patterns of Regional Evolution in England', *Transactions of the Royal Historical Soc.*, 5th series, vol. 29, 1979, pp. 92, 108.

30  W.G. Hoskins, ed., *Exeter Militia List, 1803*, Devon and Cornwall Record Soc. and Phillimore, Chichester, 1972, pp. vii–ix.

## Chapter 5 (pp. 69–87)

1  F.J. Monkhouse and H.R. Wilkinson, *Maps and Diagrams*, Methuen, 1963, p. 351.

2  Jane E. Norton, *Guide to the National and Provincial Directories of England and Wales, excluding London, published before 1856*, Royal Historical Soc., 1950, p. 130.

3  P.M. Handover, *A History of The London Gazette 1665–1965*, H.M.S.O., 1965, p. 45.

4  P.W.J. Bartrip, 'British Government Inspection, 1832–1875: Some Observations', *The Historical Journal*, vol. 25, 1982, pp. 605–26.

5  H.B. Rodgers, 'The Lancashire Cotton Industry in 1840', *Transactions of the Institute of British Geographers*, vol. 28, 1960, pp. 135–53.

6  W.B. Stephens, 'Early Victorian Coventry: Education in an Industrial Community, 1830–1851' in Alan Everitt, ed., *Perspectives in English Urban*

*History*, Macmillan, 1973, pp. 161–83.

7 Muriel Nissel, *People Count: A history of the General Register Office*, H.M.S.O., 1987, p. 42.

8 R.W. Ambler, 'A lost source? The 1829 returns of non-Anglican places of worship', *The Local Historian*, vol. 17, 1987, pp. 483–9.

9 R.W. Ambler, ed., *Lincolnshire Returns of the Census of Religious Worship 1851*, Lincoln Record Soc., vol. 72, 1972, pp. 79, 109, 111.

10 T.S. Ashton, *Economic and Social Investigations in Manchester, 1833–1933*, 2nd ed., Harvester Press, Hassocks, 1977, pp. 13–33, 45, 62–4, 103–4.

11 *Annals of the Royal Statistical Society, 1834–1934*, Royal Statistical Society of London, 1934, pp. 56–9, 97. The St Giles-in-the-Fields report is reproduced in R. Wall, ed., *Slum Conditions in London and Dublin*, Gregg International, Farnborough, 1974.

12 V.C.H. *Warwickshire*, VIII, 1969, p. 517.

13 V.C.H. *Warwickshire*, VII, 1964, p. 333; VIII, 1969, p. 278.

14 *The Survey of London*, XXXI, The Athlone Press, 1963, p. 15; XXXVII, 1973, p. 343.

15 *The Housing Question in London*, London County Council, 1900, pp. 190–2.

16 Stephen J. Page, 'A new source for the historian of urban poverty: a note on the use of charity records in Leicester 1904–29', *Urban History Yearbook*, 1987, pp. 51–60.

## Chapter 6 (pp. 88–111)

1 V.C.H. *Gloucestershire*, XI, 1976, p. 258.

2 *Guide to the Archives Department*, Doncaster Borough Council, undated, sect. 2.1.

3 Shelagh Bond and Norman Evans, 'The process of granting charters to English boroughs, 1547–1649', *English Historical Review*, vol. 91, 1976, pp. 102–20.

4 Public R.O. PC 1/883–8, 897A.

5 N.M. Herbert et al., *The 1483 Gloucester Charter in History*, Sutton, Gloucester, 1983, pp. 9–15, 52–63.

6 Philip Styles, *Studies in Seventeenth Century West Midlands History*, Roundwood Press, Kineton, 1978, p. 45.

7 John West, *Town Records*, Phillimore, Chichester, 1983, pp. 196–205 has a gazetteer of Improvement Acts and Municipal Incorporations.

8 Barbara Green and Rachel M.R. Young, *Norwich the growth of a city*, Norwich Museums, 1972, p. 22. Joyce Ellis, 'A dynamic society: social relations in Newcastle-upon-Tyne 1660–1760' in Peter Clark, ed., *The Transformation of English Provincial Towns 1600–1800*, Hutchinson, 1984, pp. 202–6.

9 H. Owen and J.B. Blakeway, *A History of Shrewsbury*, I, 1825, pp. 377–8.

10 M.G. Hobson and H.E. Salter, eds., *Oxford Council Acts 1626–1665*, Oxford Historical Soc., 1933, p. 140.

11 Shelagh Bond, ed., *The Chamber Order Book of Worcester 1602–1650*, Worcestershire Historical Soc., new series, 8, 1974, p. 40. Historical

Manuscripts Commission, *Fourteenth Report, appendix VIII, Manuscripts of Lincoln Corporation*, H.M.S.O., 1895, p. 97.

12 J. Charles Cox, ed., *The Records of the Borough of Northampton*, II, 1898, p. 453.

13 K.A. MacMahon, ed., *Beverley Corporation Minute Books (1707–1835)*, Yorkshire Archaeological Soc., CXXII, 1958, pp. xxiv–v, 80.

14 Richard Welford, *History of Newcastle and Gateshead, volume II, Sixteenth Century*, Scott, 1885, pp. 293–9, 305–10, 476–81, 504–5.

15 Joan Thirsk and J.P. Cooper, eds., *Seventeenth-Century Economic Documents*, Clarendon Press, Oxford, 1972, pp. 413–14.

16 *Records of the Corporation of Leicester*, p. 29. Richard F. Dell, *The Records of Rye Corporation*, East Sussex County Council, 1962, p. 43.

17 V.C.H. *Oxfordshire*, X, 1972, p. 75. Edward Gillett and Kenneth A. MacMahon, *A History of Hull*, Hull University Press, 1980, p. 249.

18 *Parliamentary Papers*, 1835 XXIII (116), p. 263. Elizabeth M. Halcrow, 'Borough Records: Chamberlain's or Treasurer's Accounts', *The Amateur Historian*, vol. 2, 1956, p. 294.

19 Gloucestershire R.O., GBR 1397/1502, 1663–4.

20 Bond, 1974 op.cit., p. 68.

21 Betty R. Masters, ed., *Chamber Accounts of the sixteenth century*, London Record Soc., vol. 20, 1984, p. xxx.

22 V.C.H. *The City of York*, 1961, pp. 229–32.

23 Gloucestershire R.O., GBR 1397/1502.

24 Bond, 1974 op.cit., p. 38. V.C.H. *Oxfordshire*, X, 1972, p. 76.

25 V.C.H. *The City of York*, 1961, p. 233.

26 Gloucestershire R.O., GBR 1397/1502, 1663–4.

27 G.A. Chinnery, ed., *Records of the Borough of Leicester*, VI, Leicester University Press, 1967, pp. 45–6.

28 Ibid., p. viii.

29 Corfield, 1982 op.cit., p. 156.

30 Bryan Little and Herbert Werba, *St Ives in Huntingdonshire*, Adams & Dart, Bath, 1974, p. 48.

31 *Parliamentary Papers*, 1835 XXV (116), pp. 1653–4. Harold J. Laski, W. Ivor Jennings and William A. Robson, eds., *A Century of Municipal Progress 1835–1935*, Allen & Unwin, 1935, p. 109.

32 V.C.H. *Warwickshire*, VIII, 1969, p. 273.

33 W.A. Champion, 'The frankpledge population of Shrewsbury, 1500–1720', *Local Population Studies*, no. 41, 1988, pp. 51–60.

34 Oxford University Archives, W.P. Q 9, 10. I am grateful to the Keeper of the University Archives for allowing me to consult this material.

35 Adrienne Rosen, 'Winchester in transition, 1580–1700' in Peter Clark, ed., *Country towns in pre-industrial England*, Leicester University Press, 1981, pp. 180–2.

36 Ellis, loc.cit., pp. 207, 224.

37 R.S. Neale, *Bath 1680–1850: A Social History*, Routledge & Kegan Paul, 1981, p. 69.

38 Margaret J. Hoad, ed., *Borough Sessions Papers 1653–1688*, Portsmouth Record Series, I, 1971.

39  Gloucestershire R.O., GBR 1445/1567, unfol., Michaelmas 1640.
40  Devon R.O., ECA Bk 11, p. 274. Bristol R.O., City Records, Sessions Order Book 1653–71, f. 151. Historical Manuscripts Commission, *Thirteenth Report, Appendix IV, Manuscripts of the Corporation of Hereford*, H.M.S.O., 1892, pp. 346–7, 349. Corfield, 1972 loc.cit., p. 271.
41  Styles, op.cit., pp. 244–5.
42  Alan Everitt, 'The Marketing of Agricultural Produce' in Joan Thirsk, ed., *The Agrarian History of England and Wales, IV, 1500–1640*, Cambridge University Press, 1967, p. 488.
43  Ibid., p. 541.
44  Martin Weinbaum, *British Borough Charters 1307–1660*, Cambridge University Press, 1943, pp. 8, 44, 53.
45  V.C.H. *Oxfordshire*, IV, 1979, pp. 338–9.
46  V.C.H. *Gloucestershire*, IV, 1987, p. 116; *Yorkshire, East Riding*, I, 1969, p. 439.
47  Alan D. Dyer, *The City of Worcester in the sixteenth century*, Leicester University Press, 1973, p. 208.
48  Herbert, op.cit., p. 13. Weinbaum, op.cit., p. 66.
49  Neale, op.cit., p. 92.
50  V.C.H. *Gloucestershire*, IV, 1987, p. 147. Robert Newton, *Eighteenth-Century Exeter*, The University of Exeter, 1984, p. 42.
51  James L. Bolton and Marjorie M. Maslen, eds., *Calendar of the Court Books of the Borough of Witney 1538–1610*, Oxfordshire Record Soc., LIV, 1985.
52  Dyer, op.cit., p. 204. *Records of the Corporation of Leicester*, p. 47.

## Chapter 7 (pp. 112–28)

1  J.S. Cockburn, *A History of English Assizes 1558–1714*, Cambridge University Press, 1972, p. 339.
2  *Acts of the Privy Council, 1558–1570*, 1893, pp. 323, 344, 347, 349–50; *1577–1578*, 1895, pp. 27–8, 91; *1619–21*, 1930, pp. 45, 50, 75. Historical Manuscripts Commission, *Corporation of Hereford*, loc. cit., p. 340.
3  K.J. Lindley, 'Riot Prevention and Control in Early Stuart London', *Transactions of the Royal Historical Soc.*, fifth series, vol. 33, 1983, pp. 110–11.
4  *Acts of the Privy Council 1630–1631*, 1964, p. 182.
5  *Acts of the Privy Council 1616–1617*, 1927, p. 35.
6  *Acts of the Privy Council 1629–1630*, 1960, pp. 398–9.
7  Charles Henry Cooper, *Annals of Cambridge*, II, Cambridge, 1853, p. 398.
8  *Acts of the Privy Council 1618–1619*, 1929, pp. 401, 462–3.
9  S.K. Roberts, 'Alehouses, brewing, and government under the early Stuarts', *Southern History*, vol. 2, 1980, pp. 49–50.
10  Cockburn, 1972 op.cit., pp. 153–87.
11  *Acts of the Privy Council 1619–1621*, 1930, p. 345. Public R.O., ASSI 2/1, f. 10. Cockburn, 1972 op.cit., pp. 180, 333–9.
12  J.S. Cockburn, ed., *A Calendar of Western Circuit Assize Orders, 1629–48*, Camden Soc., 4th series, 17, 1976. T.G. Barnes, ed., *Somerset Assize Orders 1629–40* and J.S. Cockburn, ed., *Somerset Assize Orders 1640–59*, Somerset Record Soc., LXV, LXXI, 1959, 1971.

13  *Calendar of State Papers, Domestic*, 1691–1692, 1900, pp. 80–264.
14  T.S. Willan, *The inland trade*, Manchester University Press, 1976, pp. 123–6.
15  *Journal of the House of Commons*, XI, pp. 605, 621, 707; XII, pp. 47, 60, 281, 551.
16  *Parliamentary Papers*, 1852–3 VIII (376), (382); 1853 (453); 1857–8 IX (387).
17  *Parliamentary Papers*, 1888 XXII (15); 1886 XXI (9); XXII (10).
18  William Brown, ed., *Yorkshire Star Chamber Proceedings*, III, Yorkshire Archaeological Soc. Record Series, LI, 1913, p. 129. D.M. Palliser, 'Civic Mentality and the Environment in Tudor York', *Northern History*, vol. XVIII, 1982, p. 93.
19  I.S. Leadam, ed., *Select Cases Before . . . The Court of Star Chamber, II, 1509–1544*, Selden Soc., XXV, 1911, pp. 142–65. Herbert, op.cit., p. 58.
20  V.C.H. *Yorkshire, East Riding*, I, 1969, p. 97.
21  Paul L. Hughes and James F. Larkin, eds., *Tudor Royal Proclamations*, 3 vols., Yale University Press, New Haven, 1964–9. James F. Larkin and Paul L. Hughes, eds., *Stuart Royal Proclamations*, I, Clarendon Press, Oxford, 1973. James F. Larkin, ed., *Stuart Royal Proclamations*, II, Clarendon Press, Oxford, 1983.
22  Public R.O., STAC/8/30/17; 8/212/3.
23  J.S. Cockburn, ed., *Calendar of Assize Records, Home Circuit Indictments Elizabeth I and James I*, 11 vols., H.M.S.O., 1975–85.
24  Public R.O., C/10/287/49.
25  Sir Thomas Smith, *De Republica Anglorum*, 1583 edn., p. 54.
26  C.W. Chalklin, *The Provincial Towns of Georgian England*, Edward Arnold, 1974, p. 192.
27  F.J. Fisher, 'The Development of the London Food Market, 1540–1640' in E.M. Carus-Wilson, ed., *Essays in Economic History*, I, Edward Arnold, 1954, pp. 146–50.
28  Francis Sheppard, *Robert Baker of Piccadilly Hall and his heirs*, London Topographical Soc., 127, 1982.
29  Everitt, 1967 op.cit., p. 476.
30  Public R.O., E 134, 3 Jas. I, E 20; E 134, 18 Jas. I, E 1; E 126/12 Trin. 26 Chas. II, 6 July.
31  J.S.W. Gibson, 'Trouble over Sheep Pens', *Cake & Cockhorse*, vol. 7, 1977, pp. 35–48.
32  V.C.H. *Warwickshire*, II, 1908, pp. 308, 345, 351. George Griffith, *History of the Free-Schools, Colleges, Hospitals, and Asylums of Birmingham*, 1861, p. 26.

## Chapter 8 (pp. 129–40)

1  Peter Borsay 'The English urban renaissance: the development of provincial urban culture c.1680–c.1760', *Social History*, vol. 5, 1977, pp. 581–603.
2  James Walvin, *Leisure and Society 1830–1950*, Longman, 1978, p. 6.
3  Charles Phythian-Adams, 'Ceremony and the citizen: the communal year at Coventry 1450–1550' in Clark and Slack, 1972 op.cit., pp. 70–80.

4 Hobson and Salter, op.cit., pp. 406–7. M.G. Hobson, ed., *Oxford Council Acts 1666–1701*, Oxford Historical Soc., 1939, pp. 126–7, 221, 264–5, 288.

5 Corfield, 1982 op.cit., p. 88.

6 Sir Francis Hill, *Georgian Lincoln*, Cambridge University Press, 1966, p. 244.

7 James Walvin, *English Urban Life 1776–1851*, Hutchinson, 1984, pp. 161–2.

8 Peter Borsay, '"All the town's a stage": urban ritual and ceremony 1660–1800' in Clark, 1984 op.cit., p. 247.

9 V.C.H. *Berkshire*, II, 1907, p. 296.

10 J.P. Earwaker, ed., *The Court Leet Records of the Manor of Manchester, II, 1586–1618*, 1885, pp. 239–40.

11 Walter Rye, ed., *Extracts from the Court Books of the City of Norwich, 1666–1688*, 1905, p. 157.

12 Devon R.O., ECA 65, General Sessions Book, 1660–72, ff. 355–6.

13 Phythian-Adams, 1972 loc.cit., p. 79. Jack Simmons, *Leicester: The Ancient Borough to 1860*, Sutton, Gloucester, 1983, p. 85. V.C.H. *Oxfordshire*, X, 1972, pp. 14, 97–8.

14 J.H. Bettey, *Wessex from AD 1000*, Longman, Harlow, 1986, p. 177.

15 Hobson and Salter, op.cit., pp. 19, 366.

16 Peter Clark, 'The Alehouse and the Alternative Society' in Donald Pennington and Keith Thomas, eds., *Puritans and Revolutionaries*, Clarendon Press, Oxford, 1978, pp. 47–72, and see the same author's *The English Alehouse: a social history 1200–1830*, Longman, Harlow, 1983.

17 *Records of the Borough of Nottingham*, V, 1625–1702, 1900, pp. 352–3.

18 Borsay, 1984 loc. cit., pp. 228–9. Historical Manuscripts Commission, *Thirteenth Report, Appendix pt. II, Calendar of the Manuscripts of the Duke of Portland II*, H.M.S.O., 1893, p. 270.

19 Defoe, op.cit., pp. 73–4, 76–7, 520.

20 Meekings et al., op.cit., pp. 24–5.

21 Hill, op.cit., pp. 3–75.

22 V.C.H. *Warwickshire*, VIII, 1969, p. 508. F. Blomefield, *An Essay towards a Topographical History of the County of Norfolk*, II, 1805, p. 443.

23 Historical Manuscripts Commission, *Report on the Manuscripts of the late Reginald Rawdon Hastings, Esq.*, II, H.M.S.O., 1930, p. 279.

24 John Beresford, ed., James Woodforde, *The Diary of a Country Parson*, III, Clarendon Press, Oxford, 1927, pp. 49–51.

25 John Whyman, 'A Hanoverian Watering-Place: Margate before the Railway' in Everitt, 1973 op.cit., pp. 142–3.

26 Jack Simmons, ed., Robert Southey, *Letters from England*, Sutton, Gloucester, 1984, p. 164.

27 Sarah Quail, 'Southsea: The Archives of the Seaside', *Archives*, vol. XVIII, 1988, pp. 208–13.

28 Walvin, 1978 op.cit., pp. 13, 69–70, 81–2. H.C. Darby, ed., *A New Historical Geography of England after 1600*, Cambridge University Press, 1976, p. 291.

29 T.W. Freeman, H.B. Rodgers and R.H. Kinvig, *Lancashire, Cheshire and the Isle of Man*, Nelson, 1966, p. 241.

30 J.E. Vaughan, *The English Guide Book c.1780–1870*, David & Charles, Newton Abbot, 1974, pp. 62–91.

31 John K. Walton, *The Blackpool Landlady. A social history*, Manchester University Press, 1978, pp. 30–1.

32 J. Whyman, 'Visitors to Margate in the 1841 census returns', *Local Population Studies*, no. 8, 1972, pp. 19–38.

33 Neil McKendrick, John Brewer and J.H. Plumb, *The Birth of a Consumer Society. The Commercialisation of Eighteenth-century England*, Hutchinson, 1983, pp. 277–8.

34 G.A. Cranfield, *The Development of the Provincial Newspaper 1700–1760*, Clarendon Press, Oxford, 1962, pp. 19–22.

35 H.E. Meller, *Leisure and the Changing City, 1870–1914*, Routledge & Kegan Paul, 1976, p. 63.

36 Bernard Rudden, *The New River, A Legal History*, Clarendon Press, Oxford, 1985, p. 145.

37 John Duncumb, *Collections towards the History and Antiquities of the County of Hereford*, I, Hereford, 1804, p. viii.

# BIBLIOGRAPHY

The urban history background is covered in a number of works, with differing approaches: S. Reynolds, *An Introduction to the History of English Medieval Towns* (Clarendon Press, Oxford, 1977); C. Platt, *The English Medieval Town* (Secker and Warburg, 1976); M. W. Beresford, *New Towns of the Middle Ages* (Lutterworth Press, 1967); P. Clark and P. Slack, *English Towns in Transition, 1500–1700* (Oxford University Press, 1976); J. Patten, *English towns, 1500–1700* (Dawson, 1978); P. J. Corfield, *The Impact of English Towns 1700–1800* (Oxford University Press, 1982); J. Walvin, *English Urban Life 1776–1851* (Hutchinson, 1984); A. Briggs, *Victorian Cities* (Penguin, 1968); H. J. Dyos and M. Wolff, eds., *The Victorian City: Images and Realities*, 2 vols. (Routledge, 1973); and P. J. Waller, *Town, City, and Nation 1850–1914* (Oxford University Press, 1983).

Introductions to local history, discussing methodology and sources, are provided in A. Rogers, *Approaches to Local History* (Longman, 1977), P. Riden, *Local History. A Handbook for Beginners* (Batsford, 1983) and W. G. Hoskins, *Local History in England* (3rd edn, Longman, 1984).

J. West, *Town Records* (Phillimore, 1983) deals with a number of sources for urban history, with useful lists, and a series of short articles appeared in *The Local Historian* between 1971 and 1975 under the heading of 'Sources for urban history'. W. B. Stephens, *Sources for English Local History* (2nd edn, Cambridge University Press, 1981) is wider ranging but has much that is useful for the urban historian, and J. J. Bagley, *Historical Interpretation 2: Sources of English History 1540 to the Present Day* (Penguin, 1971) is also informative and enjoyable. P. Riden, *Record Sources for Local History* (Batsford, 1987) deals with the Public Record Office's resources. Also helpful are a number of articles in the collection from *History* edited by L. M. Munby as *Short Guides to Records* (The Historical Association, undated).

There are comparatively few books on specific sources, although maps and plans have been well covered in P. Hindle, *Maps for Local History* (Batsford, 1988), D. Smith, *Maps and Plans: For the Local Historian and Collector* (Batsford, 1988), which has a good bibliography, and two collections of articles by J. B. Harley issued as *The Historian's Guide to Ordnance Survey Maps* and *Maps for the Local Historian* (Standing Conference for Local History, 1964 and 1972). R. Hyde, *Gilded Scenes and Shining Prospects: Panoramic Views of British Towns, 1575–1900* (Yale University Press, 1985) has an informative introduction. Deeds are explained in A. A. Dibben, *Title Deeds* (The Historical Association, 1971) and N. W. Alcock, *Old Title Deeds. A guide for local and family historians* (Phillimore, 1986), and the national censuses in E. Higgs, *Making Sense of the Census* (H.M.S.O., 1989).

The introductions to volumes issued by the record societies can provide helpful explanations of the types of documents they contain. Volumes published in many such series are usefully summarized in the two volumes of *Texts and calendars: an analytical guide to serial publications* edited by E. L. C. Mullins (Royal Historical Society, 1978 and 1983).

Articles on sources and methodology appear from time to time in periodicals. Many useful ones are to be found in *The Local Historian* and *Local Population Studies*. The journals of local historical societies should also be consulted. The periodical literature can be approached through G. H. Martin and S. McIntyre, *A Bibliography of British and Irish Municipal History* (Leicester University Press, 1972) and the annual bibliographies in *The Urban History Yearbook* (Leicester University Press, 1974–), which also contains articles and information for urban historians.

# Index